Without question the two greatest requirements of my profession are keeping current with the literature of the field and transferring the skills and knowledge of my subject to my students. It is a priviledged profession because there is nothing that I enjoy more than my subject with the possible exception of watching my students exceed not only their initial expectations but my own poor abilities as well.

I love teaching and I appreciate good teachers because I know how rare the really good ones are. That might be the right way to introduce Mark to you because he is one of the best that I have been priviledged to watch and learn from but let me begin just a bit differently.

As a teacher I can and have recommend Mark without the slightest reservation. I have witnessed and marveled many times at Mark's abilities as a teacher. The very young and the very old respond to him like no one else. That is probably his greatest gift. But it is a gift that he works at continuously, constantly seeking to improve. He cares about his craft and he cares but those he works with. Good is never good enough.

This poor preface is not really about Mark the teacher, however. It is about a man, hope, perseverance, faith, humor and hard work. It's not really self help, inspiration, or even a how to manual. Right now it is just another book that you picked up and think you should read but there are a lot of books out there all demanding your attention.

There are books of action, adventure, political tripe and self improvement. They are all competing for your attention and your time. The odds are that you already have a pile that has been collecting dust for years. They are all waiting for you to have the time that you never will and the pile is growing. Fine.

Make time for this book. This book is about personal triumph and more than how to do it. This book is about the personal reward of not quiting when quiting would be so damn easy. It is about not just winning but then sharing and helping others. It is too good to be true except that it is true.

I know Mark and I have watched his progress for many years. More importantly I have watched Mark work with my son when no one else could. My son's success is not unique. I have watched Mark work his magic with others.

Read his book.

-Dr. William Breslove PhD
Faculty, Point Park University School of Business

Overcoming the Odds:
The Mark Haffner Story

A self-help guide toward helping you and your loved
ones through life's challenging phases

By: Mark Haffner and Lionel Levine

authorHOUSE®

AuthorHouse™
1663 Liberty Drive, Suite 200
Bloomington, IN 47403
www.authorhouse.com
Phone: 1-800-839-8640

First published by AuthorHouse 7/7/2008

ISBN: 978-1-4343-8825-4 (sc)

Printed in the United States of America
Bloomington, Indiana

This book is printed on acid-free paper.

I want to dedicate this book to my loving wife Shelly, and to my beautiful and amazing daughter Lauren. I would also like to dedicate it to my brother Barry and his wife Dani, both positive role models for me throughout life. Finally I would like to dedicate this to Judy and Harold, the greatest parents anyone could ever have.

Table of Contents

PART 1:
Parenting

Chapter 1:
The Early Years

In this chapter:

Story- Infancy through Eighth Grade

Lessons- Personalize Education

-Listen to Your Child

-Let Kids Be Kids

The Early Years

During quiet shifts, when they have run out of the usual topics to discuss, maternity ward nurses occasionally play a game where they try to predict the kind of lives their newborn charges are going to lead. "That quiet one in the back," one points, "he'll be a writer." "Look at the gleam in that girl's eyes," the other nurse comments, "she'll give her parents loads of trouble." The loudest babies are always invariably written off as radio broadcasters, but for the rest, the nurses' imaginations run wild. They are policemen, lawyers, doctors, actors, and models. It is the beauty of youth, the excitement of a future unknown and a course unchartered. For these children, anything is possible. In that ward could lay a future president, a future Pulitzer Prize winner, a Nobel Laureate; the nurses' imaginations are the only limitation to their potential. I have often wondered if I was subjected to this game, if the nurses looked at me and prophesized my fate; I wonder if they came even close to the truth.

I was born a healthy and normal baby, weighing in at a healthy six pounds, seven ounces. Nothing of my birth would suggest the struggles that lay in store for me. It wasn't until I was about six weeks old that I began exhibiting troubling symptoms. To this day, I suspect that the *Mo'el* (circumciser in Hebrew) had failed to use proper sterilization techniques when he operated on me.

It was my mother who first recognized that something was wrong and called the family physician, stating something just wasn't right with me. Upon examining me, the doctor thought nothing was seriously wrong with me and prescribed penicillin. Call it mother's intuition, but my mother knew something was wrong, so she drove me to the hospital and asked that another physician examine me. He found me unresponsive and lethargic and, alarmed, immediately referred me for further tests. My poor mother was hysterical upon hearing this, but the doctor assured her that this was what had to be done and that I would be well taken care of.

In the hospital they conducted numerous tests and discovered significant fluid buildup in the meninges (external membranes that surround and protect the central nervous system) of my brain. A spinal tap would confirm the horrible truth: at six weeks old, I had developed Meningitis, a potentially lethal or permanently crippling infection. They immediately started me on an intensive antibiotic regimen, but discharged me a week later owing to an extremely infectious pathogen that was spreading rapidly through the hospital. In my already weakened state, the doctors feared that any new illness might prove fatal to me. As a result, I completed my recovery at home.

The challenges of my first year did not end there. In my weakened state, I was susceptible to infection and was sick constantly, even developing bronchitis at one point. Furthering my medical problems, whenever I drove through a tunnel, I would experience intense pain and pressure in my head, and my parents told me later that I would scream in pain. The doctors quickly determined that I had fluid buildup in my ears and prescribed tubes for me, which helped considerably.

My health problems eventually subsided, but they had served to set me back from my peers at the outset of life. Not surprisingly, I developed slowly as a consequence. I wasn't able to walk until about eighteen months, and speaking also took me longer than was expected.

At three, my parents enrolled me in a local nursery school. My teacher, observing my classroom performance, called my parents in to observe. They placed me in a room with a two-way mirror, allowing them to observe me; all the while, I was oblivious to their scrutiny. What they saw troubled them deeply. For the entire time I was under observation, I simply sat there, vacantly staring into space. They decided then to hold me back for a year and to have me undergo psychiatric testing.

Looking back, it is no exaggeration to say that the course of my life was decided by those tests. The potential consequences of those tests still frighten me to this day, but of course, at the time I hadn't the slightest idea of their importance. To my four-year-old self, they were simply schoolwork. In hindsight, this probably saved me; had I truly grasped their importance, I cannot imagine that I would have been able to handle the pressure.

During the late sixties and early seventies, the time when I was tested, little was known about mental disorders, and even less was understood about the needs of special education. As a consequence, children where labeled from an early age, either 'mainstream' or 'deficient' and their education was tracked accordingly, with deficient students accorded inferior classes and opportunities. To be labeled deficient in this environment would have proven a death stroke for my future. These tests were given in order to label me. Pass them and I was 'mainstream'; do poorly, and I would be forever designated 'deficient'.

What the tests showed was that I had deficient visual comprehension skills, meaning that it was hard for me to process information I received visually. I also had trouble solving higher-level quantitative problems, which made math a very challenging discipline for me growing up. Even with these deficiencies though, the decision was made: I was going to be mainstreamed, but with special classes for math and reading.

Of all the decisions made for me in my life, this one above all others established the course my life was going to follow. On the one hand, all my future troubles in academics might have been averted had I been deficiently educated. On the other hand, had I been sidelined from the outset, I would have never been given the opportunity to succeed later on in life. The challenges I faced in school were numerous (as you will soon see), but the thought that I would have never even been given the chance to face them, to either succeed or fail, frightens me to this day.

It is important to note, in light of that, that who I was and who I had the potential to be should not have changed. I was no different for having taken the test. All too often though, we allow these labels of ourselves and our children to become self-fulfilling. We begin to form our life to fit the label, rather than forming the label to fit our life. The fact that I was mainstream now did not suddenly eliminate the underlying issues that would plague my education in the years to come, and likewise, had I been declared deficient, my ability to succeed later in life would not have been in any way diminished. We will discuss this idea further in the lessons section, but for now, take this thought away: I was who I was, independent of some label.

Getting back to the story, having come to the decision that I was to be mainstreamed, I was enrolled in kindergarten. In kindergarten, I found myself unable to stay in line with the rest of my class. I would be there physically, but I never felt a part of it. I was in my own world; it felt like there existed this impenetrable divide that kept me separated from everyone else. As I often tell people when explaining this time of my life, "I did my own thing; I beat to my own tune."

My parents, concerned about my behavior, took me to see a psychologist. The psychologist prescribed the cure-all of behavior medications, Ritalin, in an attempt to control my impulses. I took it for a while but did not like the way the drug made me feel, so I complained to my doctor, who then took me off the medication.

My visual deficiency manifested itself in my inability to comprehend reading. I could read an entire page perfectly but have absolutely no idea what concepts the author was trying to convey. As a result, I went to a special reading class while the rest of the class worked on reading. I had also developed a speech impairment and was unable to formulate Rs and Ss properly. I was given a special speech tutor for this and found the first medium where I truly excelled. The one-on-one teaching style, taught in a low stress environment, allowed me to flourish as I never had until that point. With her help, my speech impairment was cured.

The success with my tutor contrasted heavily with the poor performance in my mainstream classes. I was a slow learner and struggled to grasp concepts that other kids seemed to understand instantly. I felt this was profoundly unfair and often acted out in class, feeling that if I couldn't understand something, neither should anyone else. It wasn't that I did not enjoy learning; on the contrary, whenever I understood something, I was eager and excited to learn. The problem was that this occurred so infrequently.

We have this unfortunate tendency to simply label children as troublemakers and seek to control them and prevent them from misbehaving. What is too often overlooked by parents and teachers is why these children misbehave in the first place. Disciplining a child after the fact is one approach; understanding why the behavior arises and possibly preempting it in the process is an entirely more beneficial approach. Children's psychology is an incredibly complex subject, and it is important to bear in mind that often the motives governing a child's misbehavior are as complex as the motives of an adult committing a crime. If it pays to examine motive in crime, I would suggest that misbehavior in a child should be equally scrutinized.

Take my case for instance. I misbehaved not because I didn't care about learning but on the contrary, because I cared as much as I did. It was my frustration and despair that caused me to act out. My teachers never bothered to understand this about me. Rather than seeing me as an eager yet frustrated learner, they viewed me as a child who cared little for learning and had to be controlled for the sake of the other students. As a result, the teachers set themselves in conflict with me, even though ultimately our interests were aligned. Had they realized the nature of my frustration, I have no doubt that they could have done a better job helping me through this time

One area where this played out was my learning disorder. I have since realized that I am primarily an auditory learner. If you tell me something, I have little trouble recalling it or analyzing it. My problem was visual, and unfortunately, a great deal of my instruction was done in a visual manner. My teachers were neither willing nor able to adapt the curriculum to better accommodate my needs, never bothering to understand why the system was failing me.

I also lacked the confidence many other kids enjoyed in their studies. Even when I got the answer right, I could never be sure of myself. My poor elementary school teachers endured year after year of my badgering them endlessly to ensure I was doing things correctly. This lack of confidence would plague me for much of my childhood.

My development was further hampered by a life-altering moment that occurred in the second grade. I had always had trouble making close friends and had very few people I truly felt comfortable with. One of the few close friends I had was a girl in my class. We both attended the same elementary school and ended up carpooling together. It was on these rides that an unexpected friendship blossomed. Too young to realize that girls were supposed to have cooties and had to be avoided, in her I soon found a best friend. Midway through second grade she fell ill and eventually died.

It was my first experience with death, and it affected me in ways I still have trouble putting into words. How was an eight-year-old supposed to understand death? What I can say is that I was forever changed by that experience. For months after her passing I was a complete wreck. Though I remember little of those months, my parents tell me that I required assistance on even basic tasks like getting dressed; I had become so numb to life. Till this day, I contend that a part of me died with her.

They say childhood is the best time of one's life; this certainly was not the case for me. Eight-year-old Mark was not a happy child. School angered and frustrated me. People never seemed to be able to understand me. Friendships were always difficult for me. I got jealous easily of the success of others and bitterly viewed any I felt were unfairly successful. This redirected anger of my own failings prevented me from forging many strong friendships. On top of that, I found myself constantly unable to sit still during class and now constantly acted out, either out of vengeance toward a system that no longer seemed to care, or in simple boredom and indifference to their reactions. Ritalin having already failed, they tried sending me to the school counselor, but I found him crass and uncaring, so I soon stopped attending sessions with him.

In this environment, I found myself constantly irritated and frustrated. Unfortunately, I took this frustration out on those who loved me and cared for me the most: my family and my teachers. A part of me always knew that they loved me, and a part of me always knew that I was hurting them, but anger clouded my judgment, and I struck out at those I knew wouldn't fight back. Till this day I regret the way I treated them.

It was during this time though, that I first discovered what was going to grow to become one of the great passions of my life: sports. Sports were wonderful. They provided a needed release for me, a means by which to excise all my pent-up frustration and to exert myself fully. The way medieval doctors used to bleed patients to drain them of the supposed bile in their system, sports drained me of all the anger and helplessness I felt. I loved the thrill of competition; I loved the physical exertion on my body. On the field I learned to relish success and handle the failure. To be honest, on the court I thought I was unbeatable. My confidence, so lacking in the classroom, kicked into overdrive on the fields and courts of my elementary school. To be sure, I had an exaggerated sense of my skills, but at the same time, I worked hard, and slowly I came to earn the respect I felt I deserved.

Sports also served to teach me my first great lesson in life. When I was in the fourth grade, my brother and I decided I wanted to take up ice hockey. Our parents took us out to a local ice rink where they held a weekly skate time, when local kids got to play hockey. The organizers divided the kids into two groups: beginner and advanced. My brother was placed in advanced, and naturally, I felt I should be in advanced as well. Against my strenuous objections, I was placed in beginners.

To put it mildly, I was horrible. I was so bad that an employee told my parents to not bother bringing me again; I would never have a future in hockey. My parents didn't know whether to laugh at his bluntness or cry at the insidious nature of his remark. What they decided to do was to ignore him. They knew this was something I felt passionately about, and they weren't going to let the opinions of others crush my dreams. They kept bringing me back every week, encouraging me to succeed at every step of the way. Not once did they mention the employee's snide comment to me; it wouldn't be until years later that I found out the truth about skate time.

As a post-script, I would go on to have a fairly successful career as a hockey player, and till this day, I coach the sport professionally.

Imagine though, if my parents had listened to the advice of the apparent expert, if they had simply accepted that I would never amount to anything in the sport. It would not have been unreasonable; they may have been tempted to save the money and time, spent in what was apparently a foolish endeavor, and instead enrolled me in activities deemed more appropriate for me. But they did not, for they saw in me a passion to succeed, a drive to make something of myself, one that perhaps even I didn't yet realize. They understood then that although it was going to be hard for me, I was going to succeed, and they never gave up on me.

As a coach, I am often approached by concerned parents wondering how many lessons their children will need, or if their sons and daughters will ever amount to anything in this sport. In response, I always tell them this story, and I tell them that all the talent in the world, without heart, is meaningless; but if a kid has heart, and has the drive to succeed, there's no telling how far he or she can go.

As school progressed, I continued to struggle. Athletics continued to play a central part of my life. I was a member of the volleyball and basketball teams, swam regularly, and played Little League baseball religiously. In spite of all that though, I continued to struggle, and my behavior continued to plague my teachers and family. My behavior got so bad that at one point our synagogue at the time, who had hosted my brother's Bar Mitzvah, asked my family to leave on my account. We found another one, but they took us only after sternly warning me to stay in line.

By now I was twelve and was entering the seventh grade. At the time, my elementary school went through the sixth grade, so my family had to choose where to send me to middle school. They settled on a local Catholic school. There I found myself a distinct minority, a fact I was reminded of regularly by my classmates. My religious background, coupled with the fact that I was a transfer student, made it hard for me to form friendships in this school.

I once again sought refuge in athletics—football this time. I was a smaller kid and faced constant hazing by the eighth graders as a result. Looking back, one would think I did not enjoy football, but football proved an important molder for me. On the gridiron, I first learned not to simply roll over take an insult, but rather to stand up for myself. Although it was a lesson that would still take several years to sink in, its seeds were planted under the goalposts in the back of the school.

It came time for me to prepare for my Bar Mitzvah. Having been personally expelled from one congregation already, I was determined to do well in my Bible recital. My family found me a tutor who recorded the entire reading portion onto tape. I worked hard and memorized the entire portion word-for-word and recited it to the congregation (in Hebrew) flawlessly. It was the first time I realized that my failures in education were not necessarily because I was stupid. I wasn't stupid; I simply processed information differently than others. Unfortunately, my formal education could never adapt to my way of learning, and I struggled in my studies.

In the end, I was able to wing it for most subjects and managed to squeak by academically. Simply having a middle school diploma, though, did not translate into having a middle school knowledge set. In reality, I was now years behind in most subjects, a hole from which I would never be able to climb out of. This was how I entered high school, unprepared socially, mentally, and physically for what was still to come.

The Early Years-Lessons

The world we live in a complex one. We are constantly bombarded with ideas and information. We meet new people and encounter new things every day. On its own, it can become overwhelming to have to process all this information, so we have adopted a thought pattern to compensate: we categorize. We create broad categories of people, items, and ideas that we use on every new thing we encounter. For instance, whenever you meet someone new, you automatically categorize the person. Depending on the impression the person gives you, you might file him or her under friendly, naive, competent, or sleazy. This is the notion of the first impression, and why it is so important. Whenever you meet someone, you will automatically be categorized, and once categorized, it is extremely hard to change your category.

This is not a bad thing. For instance, you have probably categorized snakes as dangerous, and as a result, whenever you encounter one, you will likely avoid it, even though a particular snake might be harmless. We have evolved this pattern recognition as a survival mechanism. Furthermore, the simple fact is that without these categories, we would be unable to handle the amount of information thrown at us.

That said, there is a sinister downside to this. In creating broad categories, a lot of individual details get lost, and we tend to treat all things in a category equally, even when, in reality, they should be treated very differently. Consider the example of health food. There are numerous foods that fall under this broad category, all of which, while technically healthy, are very different. A low-glycemic-index bagel, while technically healthy, is no salad. Within the broad category of health food there exists a gradient of foods of varying nutritional value. As a result, while all might be considered health food, it would be a mistake to view the foods the same way.

The reason I mention this is because just like we label food, we also label people; more specifically, we label students. As a child, you are thrown into two (or possibly three) categories: mainstream, deficient (or special needs), and sometimes gifted. Simply getting labeled one of these does not make you identical to those in your group. Like food, there exists gradients of student, and everyone is unique in needs and advantages. Being gifted does not mean you will not struggle in certain areas, and being deficient does not mean you cannot succeed in certain subjects. The simple fact is that every child, although labeled, is unique in both strengths and needs.

Unfortunately, our education system was never designed to understand and exploit the minute differences between students. For a long time, our schools refused to consider alternative methods of teaching, choosing instead to label anyone who didn't do well in the system as a trouble maker. We pushed for homogeneity amongst students, using a one-method-fits-all approach to education; those for whom it didn't work simply fell through the cracks.

This cookie-cutter mentality toward education, one that demands a one-method-fits-all approach, is increasingly being shown to be the fallacy that it is. All children are not the same; each child is endowed with certain strengths and weaknesses in learning, and each has a skill-set that, if recognized and utilized, would maximize that child's learning potential. As an example: some students are naturally more self-motivated than others. For them, it would be prudent to allow for more self-exploration and autonomy in study. For the students less naturally motivated, a firmer hand and a more directed study regimen is required. To force all students into one of those environments is clearly not the ideal solution.

This, however, is not a critique on schools. Teachers cannot be expected to implement twenty individual learning patterns in a single class. Rather, the responsibility falls on the parents. **Parents should recognize and understand the nature of their child and tailor their child's education to match it.** Thus it falls on the parents to make the proper choices about schooling. Looking back at my own life, I am absolutely convinced to this day that had my education been better tailored to fit me, I would have gotten much more out of it.

It is not that my parents didn't try. They worked very hard trying to drill my lessons into me, but it was like nailing a square peg into a round hole; the method was flawed and the resulting outcome was inferior. I squeaked by in school, but did so primarily by winging it in many subjects. I fell hopelessly behind but was graduated anyway. I thus approached high school completely unprepared, both socially and academically, for what was to come.

So my first advice would be to truly figure out what works and what doesn't for your child. Just because your child is labeled special needs does not mean placing him in special needs classes are the answer. Likewise, a kid labeled mainstream (as I was!) might still often struggle in courses. **Talk to your kid; find out what works and what doesn't. Place your child in environments where your child is most likely to succeed. Most important, if your child needs help, do not let perceived stigmas prevent him or her from receiving it.**

The second piece of advice I would have for parents is to **talk with your kids, not only at them.** My parents were involved: they cared for me, they loved me, and they wanted to see me succeed. The problem is they did not always know what it was I needed. Parents, you are correct in thinking that with age comes experience, experience that translates into knowledge, but it would be a mistake to think that knowledge infallible.

As we discussed in the story, children are complicated people with complex motivations. As a parent, it would be a mistake to overlook their motives, as understanding them is often key to resolving the issue. That is why it is so important to understand what motivates your children, and this is best accomplished simply by listening to them. For instance, if your child is misbehaving in class, it's not enough to simply rebuke him or her; instead, take the time to understand what really caused the behavior. Aside from fostering a better bond with your children, it will help you as a parent, armed with your knowledge and experience, to best assist your children during this early stage of life. For instance, had my parents and teachers understood the reasons that motivated my misbehaving in class, their responses to me would have been very different; they would have understood the problem and been able to properly address it.

The final thought I want to explore in this chapter is the phrase often used, one that urges us to **let kids be kids.** Psychologists have long theorized that playing is an innately instructive behavior, meant for kids to explore different jobs and roles, to learn by experimenting. Indeed, this age is a crucial one for developing tastes and discovering passions. The skills might not emerge until later in life, but the seeds will be planted early on.

Sports were to become my life's work, one of my driving passions. Although I could not know it at the time, it was now, at this early age, that I would first get introduced to what would later help to define me. Of course at the time all it was was a game, but it would grow to be so much more.

All games have that potential. From playing Cops and Robbers (hopefully not the robbers) to the junior chemistry set, these games will allow your children to explore the world around them. In the process of playing, they will discover their passions and uncover their talents. They will discover what they enjoy and what they hate. **The classroom isn't the only venue where they'll learn; every game is a lesson to them.**

In an age of hyper-competitiveness, where kids are pushed to read by four, know multiplication by six, and attend piano practice every afternoon; in a world where parents seem to feel that the only way for their children to get ahead is to turn them into adults as quickly as possible; in a time where playgrounds are sanitized and kids are no longer allowed to play on the street, **I urge you to let your kids play.**

No other species has such a long maturation process, and I would suggest to you that this is not a coincidence. We have evolved a complex society, complete with intricate mannerisms and customs. It only takes a couple of years to learn how to be a lion, but it takes almost twenty years (and often more) to learn how to be human. **Let kids be kids.** Let them play and enjoy themselves. Every game, every hobby, every outing, teaches them a little more about themselves and what it means to be human. There is plenty of time to be an adult; let your children relish this precious time.

To recap the lessons from this chapter:

- **Take the time to identify your children's individual strengths and weakness and construct a learning environment that will best suit them.** Don't count on teachers to do this; you know your children best. Put them in environments where they will best be able to succeed.

- **Make sure to listen to your child.** Don't assume you understand everything about them. Create an environment where they will feel comfortable opening up to you. It will foster a closer bond and will allow you to identify and properly handle whatever challenges they might face.

- **Let kids be kids.** Through games and hobbies, your children will learn much about themselves and who they will later want to be. Games aren't a luxury; they are a necessity. Allow them the time to be kids; they will be adults soon enough.

Chapter 2:
High School

In this chapter:

Story-High School
Lessons-Respect Your Child's Autonomy
-Prioritize When to Intervene
-Set the Example
-Find Mentors for Your Child

High School

Imagine a Nebraskan farm boy who decides one day he wants to see New York City. Having never left home before, he is understandably very excited at the prospect of seeing the Big Apple. So he works extra shifts, saves up, and purchases a ticket.

As he boards the train, he is overcome by fatigue (perhaps having overworked to earn the money) and immediately falls asleep. He proceeds to sleep the entire trip away, snoring through the Great Plains and snoozing through the Midwest. He awakens only to discover that he has arrived in Grand Central Station. Being thrust out onto the platform with little warning, he is immediately exposed to the intensity and bustle of the great city. The noise is deafening, and he is suddenly drowned in a sea of people. Adjectives like *overwhelmed* and *deluged* probably wouldn't do justice to what he feels at that moment. What he feels like at that moment is kind of what walking into high school on my first day of class freshman year felt like.

I had never appreciated just how sheltered I had been until that point. Up until then, I had always attended small, well-funded institutions, filled with milder suburban children. Now I found myself in a large inner-city high school, a small fish in a very big pond.

I suspect freshman year is awkward for many people, but this was especially true for me. I had yet to develop confidence in my interpersonal skills; I had yet to be successful in athletics, my enduring passion, and academics continued to mercilessly challenge me.

In some ways, my confidence was further worsened by my older brother. He was, in short, everything I was not. He was intelligent, outgoing, popular, a ladies' man, and, worst of all, he was naturally athletic. He was a city star in not one, but two sports. He was a big man on campus, and I was a forgotten shadow; his successes seemed to make my failures even worse by comparison.

I wanted nothing more than to be my older brother. I remember longingly watching him interact with friends from afar, wishing I had that natural ease and confidence he seemed to exude. In younger sibling fashion, I tried tagging along with him, but he avoided me like the plague.

But though my brother caused me a lot of envy, my brother's influence on me was not as negative as I paint it. While it was true that he did avoid me for the most part, he was always there for me when I needed him most. As a smaller kid I was subjected to bullying fairly often. My brother and his friends always made sure that I was protected, often putting would-be bullies in their place.

Furthermore, I came to idolize my brother. This worship of him would have a profoundly positive impact on me. Though his successes did serve to remind me of my failures, in doing so, they would help motivate me to succeed. That I wanted nothing more than to be like my brother often pushed me to try even harder and inspired me to never throw in the towel.

This is perhaps the greatest thing my brother ever did for me. High school is a very trying time for a person, and it is very easy, especially for students who struggle, to fall in with the wrong crowd and to start emulating the wrong sort of people. Finding the right role models is crucial for a child's development at this stage. It is at this point that a child looks around and starts deciding what sort of person he wants to be. I was lucky; I settled on wanting to be my brother. What if I had settled on someone else, though, someone with less reputable character traits? What sort of story would I be writing now had I chosen poor idols? Parents take note: this is perhaps the biggest lesson I have taken from this time in my life.

To any parent of a teenager, you are well aware that by now the direct influence you have over your child has eroded significantly. By now, he or she has chosen his or her own role models to emulate, usually from among his or her peers or older kids. We will talk more extensively about role models in the lessons section of this chapter—why they arise and what is the best role for a parent during the teenage years, but for now, I'll state this:

Should your child settle in with honorable, kind, studious, and ambitious role models, you will have little to worry about. He or she is almost guaranteed to turn out well. Should he choose a troubling set of friends, you must make every effort to maneuver better influences into his life. Again, we will talk about this more extensively later.

For my freshman year I was placed in all remedial classes. I worked hard in these and ended the year with a respectable 2.6 GPA. My academic problems did not really surface until sophomore year, when my gaps in education finally caught up with me. I took Basic Algebra and struggled heavily; that I passed was more on account of an act of kindness on my teacher's part than my deserving. I also struggled through Biology and English 2, and it was this year that I first failed a course: French.

In junior year, my academic challenges were worsened by an event that occurred in my Earth and Space class. One day, at the end of class, while I was gathering my things, a burly football player with a reputation for bullying approached me. Having never spoken to the guy before, I was surprised when he first confronted me. Making sure the teacher was out of earshot, he leaned in and let me know that he expected me to bring him five dollars tomorrow. Were I to forget, he warned me, he would "mess me up."

I should have stood up to him. I should have told an authority figure. At the very least, I should have told someone. What I did was stop attending class. I still went to school every day, but during this class period, I would skip school and go to my grandmother's and nap. She loved me in the unconditional sort of way grandparents do and never once told my parents where I went every day.

Eventually though, the school realized I was perpetually skipping class and called my parents in to a conference on my behavior. I was directly asked why I skipped, and I should have been honest, should have told them about the player (who was later expelled for, shockingly, violence in school), but having kept the secret for so long, I could not bring myself to tell them the truth and was punished severely.

Now the principal at the time was the sort of no-nonsense administrator Hollywood movies always like to portray principals as. He was brought in to restore order to a school that had lived through the ravages of the seventies, and bring order he did. One did not wear a hat in school around this man and ever hope to see it again, and God help you if he ever caught you skipping class. Luckily though, he seemed to take a liking to me and wanted to see me graduate. As a result, he assigned me a counselor whom I was to report to between every class and who was charged with verifying that I was in constant attendance.

The woman he chose was the special ed teacher at the time. Though I first hated and resented what I felt was a forced infringement on my freedom, eventually I came to appreciate and even look forward to my time with her. She had worked with numerous special-needs kids before, and she seemed to implicitly understand me, and I grew to respect her as a result. She was the first authority figure I felt truly comfortable with and felt that I could openly and honestly confide in. She gave me hope in this otherwise troubling time, making me feel that I was not alone and that I mustn't give up.

Reflecting, this is the second big lesson I took from high school. One of the major things that hampered my time in high school was the fact that for much of it, I never had a mentor or counselor with whom I felt comfortable discussing things. I couldn't go to my parents, because I was worried that their opinion of me might suffer if I confided all my troubles in them, and none of my extended family was close enough with me that I felt they could truly empathize with my issues. The result was that whenever I faced a tough situation, I was forced to come to my own decisions without the advice and counsel of someone more experienced. As a result, I often made avoidable mistakes. The Earth and Space bully is an obvious example. If I simply had someone I could have talked to, someone I felt comfortable opening up to about the issues I faced, he or she would have been able to give me the advice I needed. This teacher became that mentor, but for the better part of three years, I went without one.

If you are the parent of a teenager, one of the best things you can do to help foster the development of your child is to ensure that he finds a proper mentor to help guide him through this challenging phase. This mentor can take numerous forms, from an older sibling, to a college student, to a teacher, to a clergyman, to a therapist. The only condition is that this mentor is one who the child implicitly trusts and respects, one with whom he feels completely at ease. It is important to realize that although your children do love and trust you, there are subjects they will never be comfortable discussing with you, subjects that nevertheless require discussion. In my personal experience, I know that my mentor played a significant role in turning my high school experience around and that a mentor will help make any teenager's development that much easier. This idea will again be examined more thoroughly in the lessons section.

There was one other factor that helped to turn my high school experience around; it was athletics. Hockey had become a real passion for me during this time period, and I had devoted significant time and energy to becoming proficient. The road was a difficult and disappointing one. I had tried out for two traveling teams and failed to make the roster for both of them. Nevertheless, in my junior year, I made the varsity team at my school. This would prove a transformative experience for me. Finally my years of toil and practice began to bear fruit.

I began to emerge as a leader on the team. My years of practice had afforded me an understanding of the game, which I was now able to pass on to younger players. That year we won the AA regional championship, and I felt I was a part of something successful, that I had played a role in seeing it realized, and for the first time I really began to believe in myself.

Senior year found me the leader of the team; this was a sport I had mastered, and I was now able to direct others. I posted my best year that season, scoring nine goals in twenty games as a defenseman. Over the summer, I had bulked up in an intensive weight training regimen. This newfound strength, coupled with the confidence I had gained on the rink, transformed me socially. For the first time I was able to stand up to the bullies who had pestered me throughout high school, and not surprisingly, they backed down. I also was able to ask a good friend of mine at the time to the prom, an act unthinkable to the awkward and shy kid who had walked through the main entrance of high school three years earlier.

Sports had helped to transform me, literally turning me from a boy into a man. Without sports at this juncture, I do not know that I would have matured as effectively. Although academics continued to plague me, I no longer felt as hopeless as I had. With the help of my mentor and my newfound confidence, I was able to get through successfully.

Lessons

As we have touched on in the narrative, at this stage in childhood development, parents play an increasingly indirect role in a child's formation. This does not mean that a parent cannot be incredibly influential, only that the means by which a parent exerts influence becomes much more subtle.

To a young child, his or her parents are the world, and the child will wish nothing more than to emulate them. As this child begins to mature, though, his or her outlook will likewise begin to mature, and he or she will begin to broaden perspectives. This is especially true around puberty, for it is at this time that children begin to explore what sort of person they wish to be. In this exploration of character, the child's outlook is widened, and the child will begin to seek out role models and examples from his or her surroundings whose characteristics the child finds enviable.

At this stage, a teenager cannot be viewed as a young child anymore. A parent must be able to give his or her kids significant leeway, and must allow his or her children the ability to learn and to experiment. A parent must afford his or her children the responsibility of self-discovery and realize that no child will ever respond well to having a lifestyle forced on him. This is the first major criterion I would place on proper parenting of teenagers: respect. Respect your teenagers and the decisions they make, and they will naturally respect and listen to you in turn.

I cannot emphasize this criterion enough. As a parent, I want what is best for my child, and I never want to see her make mistakes or get hurt. Therefore, I am often tempted to actively direct my daughter and guide her down what I know to be the best path. This, however, would be a grave error on my part. Part of learning always has been making mistakes and correcting them in the process. Your children will only ever be able to discover themselves if you allow them the room to experiment and the ability to make the wrong decisions. Of course, no one denies that you could do a much better job living their lives, but that is hardly the point. At the end of the day, it is their life to lead, not yours. I can assure you that if you accord them the autonomy to be themselves, they will emerge the better for it.

But there lies a real fear in allowing your children the autonomy I advocate: the fear of failure. It would be a mistake to not allow them freedom, but wouldn't it also be a mistake to simply sit back and let them fail? Obviously moderation is called for. A parent doesn't cease parental duties the moment their child becomes a teen; parental structure and guidance is still very much required.

The question then becomes, to what extent should a parent respect the autonomy of a child, and when is intervention warranted. Anecdotally, what happens if your child begins to fall in with the wrong sort, if he starts making decisions you are not comfortable with or know to be plainly wrong? Until what point do you allow him the room to make mistakes, and at what point must you step in?

This is, of course, the hardest and most delicate part of parenting, and it would be incredibly foolish of me to assume that I have all the answers to this. Nevertheless, there are several critical criteria for intervention I have settled on, criteria that every parent, myself included, should follow.

The first is to **prioritize** your interests. Although you might hold an ideal image for your children, expecting them to follow it perfectly will only result in a negative backlash toward you. Many parents unfortunately try to relive their lives through their children, correcting all their perceived mistakes in the process. This is a horrible thing to do. Parents must realize that their children are not them, and will have unique desires, interests, and motives separate from their parents'. A parent must allow each child the ability to form as an individual.

As a result I would suggest to fellow parents to learn to prioritize your child's decisions, allowing for leeway on most, but being firm on some. Don't try to mold your child, simply act to ensure your child does not get too far out of line. If you pick and choose your battles in this manner, you will be far more effective in your results.

Of course, this begs the question of how one prioritizes, and I would suggest the following criterion: **permanence**. A child should be allowed to experiment and innovate, only to the extent that the consequences aren't permanent. Once he is faced with an issue that has permanent, life-altering consequences, your intervention would be warranted. An example of this might be bodily manipulation. Should your child wish to dye his hair or get some piercings as a form of self-expression, I would recommend allowing this even if you do not approve. This is a part of his self-discovery and should be encouraged. Where I would draw the line is tattoos, a form of expression that is permanent. Here the child's decision, once made, is, for all intents and purposes, irreversible. Here your direct oversight and wisdom is required.

In a similar mold, something like education can never be compromised on. The effects of a child slacking on education will be felt throughout his life, and a parent should never allow his or her child to slack in this regard.

This test of permanence should be applied to all aspects of your child's development when the question of intervention arises. If your teenager decides he wants to discontinue his piano lessons, let him. Other than ruining his future as a concert pianist, this will not have permanent effects. On the other hand, if your child starts experimenting with narcotics or addictive substances, this is something that can have lifelong repercussions, and as such, parental intervention would be required.

This test is vague for a simple reason: each parent will prioritize and apply the test of permanence differently. There can be no absolute standard for this for the simple reason that every child will be different, and every parent will be comfortable at differing levels of teenage autonomy. But as a general standard, I think this is a good one on which to model direct intervention on the parent's part: allow for your child to develop on his own, all the while ensuring he does not make any irreparable mistakes along the way.

There is a third important parenting criterion I would suggest. Simply stated, it is to be the example you wish to see in your child. Another way of putting it: a good parent is one who **sets the example**. This seems apparent, but is often overlooked in parenting. This criterion also has several facets.

The most apparent facet is to never contradict yourself in word and action. To hold your child to a standard higher than you hold yourself will not be effective, even if you are well intentioned. The child will not perceive your actions as being in his best interests (you might be trying to keep the child away from mistakes you have made/are making); all the child will see is the apparent injustice of being denied something the parent readily takes part in. Anecdotally, imagine a smoker who tells his children not to smoke. How effective do you think this will be? The simple fact is children are easily put off by the double standard they perceive and will simply disregard their parents as authorities in the matter. Some might even revert to the behavior simply out of spite. If you want your children to stay away from certain activities, avoiding them yourself will help bolster your case.

There is a positive facet to this as well. A teenager is constantly on the lookout for examples to follow and people to emulate. Although many teenagers do not realize it themselves, this is an incredibly impressionable time for them. Simply by living a good example, you will affect your children. Likewise, by surrounding your child with numerous positive influences, you will invariably impact your child's outlook for the better. Referring back to the narrative section, you, as a parent, cannot force who your teenager idolizes, but by simply exposing your teenager to positive influences that he will respect and introducing him to potential mentors, your child will invariably come to be influenced by them.

Thus, if you are worried about the kind of crowd your teenager is beginning to hang out with or the influences your child seems to be embracing, the course of action I would recommend would be to expose him to alternative, positive influences, perhaps the best form being a mentor. What form a mentor might take will be elaborated on in conjunction with the next lesson we discuss, on the need for mentorship at this age.

This might seem like an annoyingly subtle plan, especially when you are dealing with your child. The temptation to act harshly in the hopes of seeing immediate results is an obvious and tempting desire. In the long term, though, positioning positive mentors will be hugely beneficial for your child. It may take years to see results, but your child will get molded by these influences, and they will serve to set him on the right path, long term.

This brings us to the second lesson from the narrative. Teenage years are very difficult ones, and it is essential that a teenager have some form of mentor or guidance counselor that he feels comfortable enough with to discuss the innumerable issues that arise during this time. Often, this mentor-teenager bond arises spontaneously; however, in the advent that it does not (as it didn't with me), as a parent, the best thing you can do is to locate and position someone to fill that role for your teen. Often this can take the form of an older child in the community. If you are a religious family, a youth pastor or rabbi can be called upon to serve as a mentor for your child. Barring those options, it is not a bad idea to take teenagers to a therapist, as this low-pressure environment will be conducive for them to open up about their troubles.

To recap the lessons from this chapter:

- **Respect** your children for their independence and intelligence, and do not try to micromanage their lives as a result.

- **Prioritize** the areas from which your child cannot deviate in his self-discovery process by applying the **test of permanence.** For areas that fall outside of the test, allow for flexibility.

- **Set the Example** for your children by being the sort of person you want to see your children become. This will have a powerful influence on them.

- **Find mentors** for your child to discuss issues with and who will help influence your child positively

Part 2:
Life

Chapter 3:
The College Years

In this chapter:

Story-College
Lessons-Be Your Own Best Advocate
-Focus on Ends
-Be Able to Take and Give Criticism
-Don't Let Fear Paralyze You

The College Years

The senior year of high school is one of those odd times in a person's life when his head and body exist in two completely different places. It is a time when one is physically there, but mentally, one is detached from the surroundings. Perhaps it is best compared to the day or so before Christmas holiday, when you may be at work, but your head is swimming in yuletide. For a high school senior, with one foot already out the door, there is only one thought that permeates the haze of senioritis, one word that rings throughout the halls, bouncing off lockers and floating through cafeteria lines. It is whispered in that odd combination of hope and dread, the acknowledgment that the outcome of one's life may well rest on it. It is the only thing that seems to matter to a senior; it is college.

My high school was like every other in this respect. The autumn wind blew in with it all the stresses of college applications and the SATs. It seemed the only thing my friends wanted to discuss anymore, endlessly comparing campuses, majors, and careers. Where once our discussions focused on the Steelers or the cheerleading squad, suddenly our discussions focused on city vs. rural campuses and the availability of financial aid.

Though my friends seemed eager and even anxious to encounter this new phase in their lives, I was decidedly mixed on the idea. On the one hand, I felt determined to make it in life, and I knew college was the ticket to success. In a similar vein, my brother had already been in college for a couple of years, and the idea of my not being able to follow him sickened me. On the other hand, there were the SATs.

SAT, or Scholastic Aptitude Test, is an acronym that has been given numerous other meanings by the high school kids it has tormented through the years. As the testing date approached, the only one that seemed appropriate for me was "Scary and Terrifying." Though my teachers attempted to help me in every way possible, they could only do so much, and in the end, it came down to me vs. the SAT, armed with only the two #2 pencils I brought to the testing area. What ensued was a mental bloodbath.

I had taken hard tests in my life, but few compared to the SAT. It seemed to know my weaknesses and targeted them with a merciless fury. When my parents asked me how I'd done, one look told them all they'd need to know. This test wasn't going to vindicate my years of academic struggle; it was simply going to confirm them.

So it was with dread that I awaited the results of the test. As results filtered in, my friends eagerly reported their scores: 1260, 1310, 110. My score? 800.

There is a message often repeated to kids who do poorly on standardized tests. "You are not dumb," we are told, "you are simply a bad test taker. This has no bearing on your actual intelligence." These are comforting words, but they did little to console me at the time.

Nevertheless, it's a lesson worth repeating. If a person scores well on a standardized test, all that it means is that the individual happens to be skilled at taking this particular test. We can infer intellect and skill from the results, but one's score is far from a definitive proof. There is simply no concrete causation between intellect and success on these tests. Certainly if one scores well it is usually evidence that the individual is knowledgeable in the material and is reasonably intelligent, but this is not true of everyone who takes it successfully. Likewise, scoring badly can usually be blamed on a lack of knowledge and intelligence, but there are plenty of knowledgeable and intelligent individuals who still do poorly.

If this is the case, why do we fall back on these scores so readily? The answer ties into one of the overriding themes of this book: the tendency of society to standardize and simplify. In this instance, college admissions officers need an easy way of qualitatively judging the numerous applicants they receive, in order to determine who is fit for admission. Having little personal knowledge of each applicant, admissions officers rely instead on this standardized system, which accords everyone a number by which they can be easily compared to one another. As it is generally considered accurate, the system has, by and large, been adopted. That some kids might unfairly get excluded is considered an acceptable price for the convenience of this system.

In all fairness though, I cannot criticize this system, for the simple reason that I have no better alternative to propose. Given the hundreds of thousands of applications every year, a simplification is required. To allow for a full and complete examination of every applicant would render the entire process untenable. Nevertheless, this system is not without flaws, flaws that should be recognized.

There is another, more subtle lesson I want people to take away from the SAT. While the SAT might test intelligence and knowledge, the one thing an SAT score will never be able to tell you is success. A 1600 (or 2400 now) score will not guarantee success, and an 800 will never guarantee failure. In this economy, with its diverse set of needs, there are many paths to success, and not all of them require the kind intelligence scoring well on the SAT indicates.

If you know someone who has recently scored less than he wanted on his standardized tests, make sure he understands this lesson. Though it was hard for me, as a seventeen-year-old, to believe, an SAT score will have no bearing on future success in life.

I was in a deep funk for about a week after receiving my test scores. While my friends were eagerly discussing their college options, I was convinced I now had none. My mentor helped me out of this funk, assuring me that I still had options available to me. So halfheartedly, I began researching options and ended up applying to a junior college in Cincinnati, where I was accepted.

I toyed with the idea of attending but found I was too uncomfortable with the idea of leaving home, so I began to explore local alternatives instead. As a result, I applied to a local prep school, where I had done some summer programs, for some postgraduate study. The school, knowing little about me, turned to a good friend of mine at the time, who was enrolled at the school, and asked him about me as a perspective student. As I would later find out, he flatly rejected the idea of my attending, telling the administrators that I would make a poor fit and I shouldn't be admitted.

This betrayal was one of the kindest things anyone has ever done for me. Although had I known what he did at the time, I would have undoubtedly felt abandoned and let down by someone I trusted, the truth is prep school would have been a very bad fit for me. My already struggling academic endeavors would have been overwhelmed by the intensity of a prep school environment, and a failure at this juncture might very well have resulted in my abandoning school altogether. What my friend did was not vindictive; he was motivated by a genuine desire to see me succeed, and if that meant inflicting a small insult, he was willing to do so.

My friend displayed the kind of maturity and responsibility that a true friend must. Too often we are afraid of insulting our friends and injuring their pride. As a result, we often withhold constructive and even necessary criticism. A true friend, though, must be motivated solely by seeing his or her friends succeed, and as a result, must be willing to occasionally correct them when they err. Anyone can compliment; it is the true friend who can criticize.

Facing no real alternative, I applied to community college and was accepted. Here I enrolled in all remedial courses. This turned out to be the perfect environment for me. The courses allowed me a chance to shore up some deficiencies that had existed in my education till that point, all at a relatively comfortable teaching level. They even had a special center devoted to helping students like me with learning disabilities.

I took most of my general requirements first in order to get them out of the way. The one subject that continued to plague me though was math. I attempted to take my math requirement several times in community college, but try though I might, I could not grasp the material, and facing the specter of failing, I withdrew each time. Another course that gave me trouble was remedial English. Here, though, I figured out a way to beat the system.

I managed to convince the college administrators that remedial English wasn't challenging enough for me and I should be allowed to take regular English. I then cross-registered at the University of Pittsburgh and took the course there. The instructor at Pitt was a good friend and helped me pass the class. As a result, I ended up doing better in standard English than I would have at the remedial level. It was a nice break from the trend, that in a system that seemed constantly stacked against me, I was able to twist things to my advantage, at least this one time.

I stayed in community college for two years, accumulating thirty-one credits and a respectable GPA. At this point, I finally felt ready to tackle college, so I applied and was accepted to the University of Maryland as a transfer student. The day I received my acceptance letter was one of the happiest of my life. That a nationally recognized academic institution acknowledged my work till this point and accepted me into its program was to me a vindication that all my work had not been in vain.

Not surprisingly, Maryland was a huge step up from remedial community college, and I faced a rather steep learning curve. My first semester, I struggled through the courses on my own, and ended up with a low C average. Realizing I was in need of help, I went to the Disabled Student Services and met with one of the professors who worked there. He pointedly told me that I should have attended a smaller school, where more personalized care could have been given. That said, I was at Maryland, and as of that moment, he was going to ensure that I made it through.

The doctor implicitly understood the challenges I faced and tailored my education so as to best accommodate me. He found people to take notes for me in class, allowing me to just listen to the lecturer and absorb the lesson. Exams were also administered orally, with my professors quizzing me on the material in class. When my friends started noticing my absences from class on exam days, they would ask me "Haf, where are you disappearing to?" They thought I was crazy when I told them; who would want to get personally quizzed by the professor? It seemed too intense for them. For me, though, it was the perfect system. I had always struggled on tests; the ability to communicate ideas through writing had always challenged me, but in discussion, I felt comfortable relaying answers. Thanks to this system, implemented on my behalf, I was able to do well at Maryland.

This story taught me an important lesson. Pride often prevents many people from seeking help when they need it. Many figure that to ask for help is to admit defeat, and they are not quitters, so they continue down their mistaken paths. Sometimes this takes the form of little things like asking for directions when lost; sometimes, though, this takes the form of big things, like bullying in an Earth and Space class.

The problem is that many people misperceive defeat, substituting the means for the ends. As an example of what I mean, consider driving. Your destination is the desired goal, the end if you will; how you get there is simply the means. Often though, we get so focused on the means—in driving we become obsessed with not having to ask directions because to do so would be to admit that we were incapable of finding it on our own—that we sacrifice the ends—in driving, literally arriving at the destination—in the process.

Instead, you should always focus on the desired ends and should be focused primarily on how best to meet them. If adapting the original plan or even asking someone else for assistance is required, it shouldn't be viewed with stigma, because in the end, you will be better off for having taken the necessary steps to meet the end.

In high school, this was a lesson I had yet to master, letting superficial pride interfere with my real reason for being there: an education. By the time I reached college though, maturity had afforded me this perspective, and I was able to turn to others for help when I needed assistance.

With the help of the doctor in the Disabled Student Services, my collegiate experience was improved dramatically, and I was able to settle down and actually enjoy my time. That is not to suggest that I did not work incredibly hard, only that for the first time, I felt comfortable in an academic environment, and for the first time, I felt that I could handle the rigors of school. As school continued, I was even able to land an internship in Senator Arlen Specter's office. For a kid who had only a year before been enrolled in community college, walking the halls of power in Washington DC (even if only as a memo boy) was an exciting rush.

As the year drew to a close, I declared my major, a Bachelor of General Studies. For it, I had to complete one math course: Basic College Math. The very course that had haunted my college experience returned with a vengeance, and I once more tried to take it over the summer at Pitt. Try though I might, once more I had to withdraw, having failed to grasp the material. Desperation set in on my part, I did not see how I could pass the class.

I went and spoke to one of the deans at Maryland, who assured me that, without exception, no student would be allowed to graduate without taking that math course. All my work till that point suddenly seemed worthless, I had hit a hurdle I did not seem capable of clearing.

In a panic, I once more turned to my friend in the Disabled Student Services office, and he promised to see what he could do for me. A week of anxious waiting followed. I had many sleepless nights that week, and I don't recall even eating a full meal until the doctor got back to me. They had worked out a compromise; I would have to take a philosophy class instead. Apparently, the thinking was that similar thought processes were required in philosophy and mathematics, and so long as I could prove proficient in one of the two, I would graduate.

While having to take a philosophy course was not something I was looking forward to, suddenly there was hope again. I began to see a light at the end of what had been a very long and dark tunnel.

This course however, would prove in every way as daunting as the mathematics it was meant to replace. Perhaps the only thing that made it different was that, unlike in mathematics, here, everyone struggled. I got close to many of my fellow classmates in this course as we formed many study groups in our efforts to pass the course. All our work aside, I still bombed the midterm, and fearing that this cure was no better than the disease it aimed to treat, I once again turned to my doctor friend in the DSS office. He agreed to accompany me to a meeting with the professor where he advocated my case, explaining to her that I was one semester shy of graduating, and that a failure in this class would set me irreparably back.

I wasn't looking for sympathy on the instructor's part, but neither was I expecting the sort of vindictiveness she showed me in response. The next day's lecture, she walked in and told the whole class to put their notes away for ten minutes. Then she posed a problem to the class. "Say there is a student failing this course," she began, "and he needs only this class in order to graduate from the university. Should we just give him an A even if he doesn't deserve it?" She then pretended to be genuinely interested in the answers the class gave, but it was clear that she had already accomplished all that she wanted to. She didn't have to mention my name. Enough people knew me and my story to figure out who she was talking about. I had never been so humiliated in my life.

A part of me wanted to stand up and confront her right there. Another part of me simply wanted to storm out of the lecture. My body screamed for action. "Do something, anything!" my brain shouted at me, but against every instinct, I sat there, resolved to give her no satisfaction with even the slightest reaction. Instead, I resolutely decided then and there that I would not give this woman the satisfaction of failing me.

In the following weeks, I studied with a passion and intensity I had never known before. Philosophy came no easier to me, but suddenly I was a man possessed; I was going to pass that test. The final arrived, and sure enough, I did well enough that the instructor had to pass me.

With that, I graduated from the University of Maryland with a bachelor's degree in General Sciences. Words cannot describe the pride and happiness I felt ascending the podium that sunny spring day to accept my diploma. That I, Mark Haffner, the same kid who struggled through first and second grade reading, would one day parade down a stage in cap and gown was a feat I never dreamed possible. I had worked toward it for years, but in all that time I never seriously imagined one day I would actually see my dream realized. On that sunny spring day, I was a part of a miracle. Even years later, I still tear up thinking about it.

Lessons

While high school serves to define a person's character, college primarily helps to cement a person's interests and future career path. At this stage in development, one settles on the pursuits that will define his or her life. The lessons and advice I have for this juncture revolve around how best to navigate this period of development.

You will notice that the nature of the advice shifts; I will now be focusing directly on you, not how you can best help others, but how to better yourself. The reason for this shift is that at this stage in life, your character and personality have emerged from under the direct influences of others, and you now have become the primary driver of your fate. Adapting and changing can be influenced by those around you, but you are principally responsible for ensuring your success.

So how does one best succeed at this time in his life? Reflecting on my life, I have several suggestions.

The first thing to recognize about this time is that now you will be subjected to many people defining your self-worth for you. SAT scores are one example, but college admissions, job applications, internships, and even dating are all examples of situations where you will submit yourself to others and they will rule on your worth. If they think you worthy enough, they accept you; should they find you insufficiently worthy or qualified, they reject you. In short, it will be others who will make judgments on your self-worth; it would be easy to assume this is beyond your control.

It is easy to fall into the hole of allowing others to define you, but this is a hole you must avoid. Your fundamental character does not change based on someone else's opinion. The manifestation of it might, as we will get into, but who you are fundamentally can never be defined by someone else. Anecdotally, if you receive a rejection letter one day, are you any different than you were the day before? Has that letter changed you? The simple fact is that who you are can never be redefined by someone else, unless you let it.

So let us say you do receive that rejection letter. "Sure," you'll say, "I'm not any different for receiving it. Perhaps, though, I was always a failure; I just never realized it until now. I deluded myself into thinking I might actually be a success." While it might be tempting to simply define yourself as a failure, to do this would be perhaps the worst thing you could possibly do. To accept that you are a failure is a self-destructive act and will ultimately become a self-fulfilling prophesy if you let it.

This leads me to the first advice point of the section: **be your own best advocate**.

Ultimately, no one will have as much of a vested interest in seeing you succeed as you will, for the simple reason that no one else has as much riding on your future as you do. As a result, no one will ever try as hard to see you succeed as you will. If you are unwilling to exert yourself to succeed, I can guarantee you no one else will for you. Touching on what we said before, ultimately your success in life will be defined by you.

That said, it is then important to define what exactly a rejection means. A rejection by someone else can never change who you fundamentally are; what it will change is how you realize it. If you are a talented individual, a rejection from a certain school, program, or job does not make you a failure. All it means is that you will have to find your success in other venues. If you have the ability to succeed, you will; you simply must be willing to adapt to realize it.

This is why I said earlier that a person's fundamental character will not change with rejection, but its manifestation might. Adapt to the opportunities you are given and make the most of them. Remember this: **you cannot control the opportunities you are given; what you do with them, you can control.**

This is why it is so destructive if you do not believe in yourself. If you do not believe yourself capable of succeeding, you will never allow yourself to succeed, and it will become a self-fulfilling prophesy. This is why I tell you to be your own best advocate. Believe in yourself, and ultimately you will succeed, although likely in a different form than you first imagined.

Apply this principle to your education, your career, and even your love life. Using dating as an example, if you approach women regularly, you will often be rejected, regardless of who you are. This does not make you undesirable and incapable of finding love; it simply means it won't happen with that particular woman (and since you are only meant to end up with one woman, the fact that it won't work out with most others is only natural). Now if you recognize that all a rejection from a woman means is that the two of you are incompatible, you will move on and hopefully you will eventually find love elsewhere. If, on the other hand, you internalize this rejection and feel that there is something fundamentally wrong with you, you will withdraw from the fairer sex and might very well end up alone. Your acceptance of the rejection then becomes a self-fulfilling prophesy, be it in love, education, or a career.

The second important lesson I derived from this time period was the need to put your life into perspective and **focus on the ends**. As we discussed in the story, too often in life one loses sight of what is really important and tends to get caught up in the day-to-day trivialities of how to obtain it. The driving metaphor is a good one in this regard. Too often, the perceived insult to our pride of having to ask for directions impedes our ability to arrive at our desired destination.

It is easy to conceptualize why misplaced pride can be damaging. If you allow pride to interfere with your ability to successfully accomplish goals, it is rather apparent that this pride is harmful. Logical though this might seem, it is often not applied in our day-to-day lives (we wouldn't have nearly as many lost drivers on the road if it was).

Pride can be a very damaging trait. History is filled with the anecdotes of overly proud kings and rulers whose excessive pride (often referred to as hubris) leads to their ruin. Contemporarily, we have ample examples of destructive pride interjecting itself in our lives. From being convinced that we can fix the leak in the roof, to cooking that Indian dish from memory, we let our pride get in the way of turning toward those who could help us, and disaster, or an upset stomach, is often the result.

Ridding yourself of this damaging and counterproductive pride is not easy, but if mentally you subtly redefine success, I think you can go a long way toward purging yourself of it. The problem with this pride arises when one values independence and self-reliance above all else. Don't get me wrong; these are notable traits, but focusing on them is potentially destructive. Instead, I would suggest training yourself to take pride in the ability to get something done correctly. Included in this pride would be valuing the necessary flexibility (and possible humility in turning to others) in order to see your ends realized. Accomplish this and you will have redirected your pride toward positive rather than destructive outcomes, valuing a job well done above all else.

In order to ensure that you do not fall victim to misplaced pride, I would further recommend applying the following mental test when you face a challenge. Ask yourself if the course of action you are undertaking is motivated by anything other than seeing the goal accomplished in the best possible way. If your answer is no, your action needs to be reconsidered. To summarize this idea, **never let pride interfere with your goals in life.**

Building on this idea of destructive pride, too often this pride interferes with our ability to be receptive to advice, no matter how beneficial. In the story, we discussed the need to be able to criticize a friend constructively, but more important, one has to be able to accept constructive criticism when offered. Do not let an ego or destructive pride blind you to the reality that you have areas in need of improvement. **If a friend offers**

you advice, it is in your best interest to swallow a small insult now to ensure a better you in the long run.

Your goals in life though, can get derailed by more than misplaced pride and a failure to turn to others for help when it is needed. There is another, more subtle idea that I wish to examine, one that is spoken of often but is worth repeating here.

Life is a busy and hectic experience, and we are all caught up in a rip-tide of responsibilities, obligations, and commitments. The old adage that there is ever enough time in a day has seldom been more accurate than in our hectic and chaotic society. We are swamped with teleconferences and presentations, consumed by PTA meetings and chauffeuring the kids to soccer practice. Life today seems defined by the endless amounts of work we face.

Lost under a pile of reports to file, or smothered under lists of chores to accomplish, were the ends we had set out to accomplish in our lives. In this chaotic haze that has settled on our daily routine, how often do we forget what it is that we sought to accomplish in the first place? We are so busy working, that we often forget to step back and ask ourselves, "Why? Why am I doing this? What do I hope to accomplish in completing this task? Who will benefit from my efforts?" We have become so engrossed in the means, that the ends we wanted, that we embarked on a journey to realize, have been forgotten.

This is why it is imperative to focus on the ends, the big picture, or, as the common expression would caution: **make sure to see the forest in the trees**. It is incumbent on every person to sit back from time to time and take stock of his station in life. Every person should, from time to time, ask if what he is doing is advancing him toward his desired ends. More often than not, the answer, surprisingly, will be no.

I would suggest that meditation is a useful and relaxing way of doing this. Take the time, at least once a week, to reflect on life and to take stock of where you stand and where you wish to stand. If you are not happy with where you are (and who is ever completely satisfied with his position in life?), reflect on what you could be doing differently to further you toward getting there.

All the contemplation in the world though is meaningless if it is not backed up by action. Simply realizing that you are on the wrong path will not be enough if you are unwilling to change it. This is especially true if you have invested significant time and effort into something— for instance, to obtain a degree you realize you do not need, or pursue a promotion you realize you might not really want. It might not be ideal, you will tell yourself, but you've already invested so much in obtaining it, it seems foolish to abandon it.

Furthermore, change always involves a degree of risk and it can often be a frightening undertaking. There is much uncertainty that accompanies change; and the bigger the change, the greater the uncertainty. Everyone, myself included, is risk adverse; we all, to some degree, like to hedge our bets. There is an old adage that summarizes this perfectly: **better the evil you know than the evil you don't.**

For the first concern, that you have already invested heavily in a course of action and should just see it through to the end, there is an economics term for this sort of investment: **sunk cost**. Essentially, sunk cost is the unrecoverable investment that you put into a process, should you wish to pull out. The classic example of this is waiting for a bus. It is a frigid cold night, and all your friends are staying inside. You though, decided to brave the cold and go out. Now you have been waiting at the bus stop for over twenty minutes and are frozen to the bone. Any desire you might have had to go out has long since disappeared (along with any feeling in your fingers and toes). You are tempted to just return home and warm yourself over some hot cocoa and a cheesy romantic comedy, but at the same time, you figure you have already spent twenty minutes waiting for a bus and you really don't want to have wasted that time. What should you do?

The twenty minutes you spent waiting are what economists would consider sunk cost; now, even if you go home, you will never be able to recover that time. So what do economists recommend doing here? They would tell you to ignore the sunk cost entirely. What is done is done; the only relevant question now is what do you want to do. If you still want to go out, stay, but if you have lost all desire to, go home. The twenty minutes were how you spent your time till now; they shouldn't have to define how you spend it going forward.

So if you have invested heavily in something you are now unsure you want, ignore the time and effort you have spent till this point. They are unrecoverable. The only thing they represent is what you have spent your time till now doing. Don't become a slave to them, and do not allow them to define what you must do going forward. Ask yourself only what you want going forward, and if the answer is something different, why would you continue with what you don't want?

One of the most inspiring examples I have ever encountered of this was from a dear friend of mine. She had gone to law school and become a successful practicing attorney. But twenty-some years later she found herself deeply dissatisfied with her life and career; she was not happy and did not find work as a lawyer meaningful. She had always had a passion for tea, though, and had always dreamed of opening a tea shop. And so, in her fifties, even though she had invested so much in law, she quit her job and opened a tea shop. Today, several years on, the business she runs makes her almost as much as she made as a lawyer, but more important, today she is genuinely happy.

Addressing the other concern, that any change brings risk, there is of course truth to this, and nothing I could say could possibly make the risk any less real. There is only one thing I would say on this. Any change will have risk, and the greater the change, the greater the risk of failure. My friend might have abandoned her law career only to go broke trying to make her tea shop successful. The inspiring success story might have ended very differently.

All that said, remember one thing: we are only given one chance at life; we only have one shot to get it right. There are no redos or do-overs in this game, and the stakes are nothing less than your happiness and fulfillment. We are only given one fleetingly short interval to get it right.

The simple and frightening fact is that your time here, once spent, can never be recovered. You will only be twenty, thirty, or forty once. If you are not happy now, if you feel your life is unfulfilling, you will never be able to redo it. I would suggest to you that squandering your time here is an outcome far worse than any risk. As such, if you must take some risks to bring happiness and meaning to your life, to me, it is worth the risk.

Understand that I do not recommend recklessness. My lawyer friend, for instance, did significant market research and drew up a comprehensive business model prior to quitting. Be smart and calculating in the risks you undertake, but do not be afraid to take them. **It is better to take the risks and potentially fail in the pursuit of a meaningful life than to live a life dissatisfied.**

The final piece of advice is not only that you need to be able to criticize a friend constructively, but, more important, that you be able to accept constructive criticism when offered. Once again, do not let an ego or destructive pride blind you to the reality that you have areas in need of improvement. If a friend offers you advice, it is in your best interest to swallow a small insult now to ensure a better you in the long run.

To summarize this section:

- **Be your own best advocate**. Do not internalize the rejections of others, and make the most of the opportunities you are given.

- **Focus on the ends**. Do not let a misplaced desire to succeed in the means derail your original goals, and always keep the ends in mind. Do not get lost in the day-to-day routine; make sure to see the forest in the trees.

- **Be able to give and receive helpful criticism.** Don't let the fear of a small insult get in the way of long-term improvement.

- **Don't let the fear of uncertainty and risk prevent you from making the changes you need to find happiness.** If you are unhappy, look for smart ways to find more meaning and fulfillment in life.

Remember your goals, don't get caught up in the day-to-day of attaining them, and never let pride or fear interfere with your ambitions.

Chapter 4:
Welcome to
the Corporate World

In this chapter:

Story-Starting Out on My Own
Lessons-Know Thyself
-Avoid Delusion
-Third-Person Introspection

Welcome to the Corporate World

Growing up, most people don't realize how ordered and structured their lives are. Kids go to school at eight in the morning, come home at four, and do their homework at night. Their summers are reserved first for camp, and later for summer jobs. Assignments are handed to them, and deadlines are clearly set. Success is likewise clearly delineated in the form of grades. At all times children know exactly what is expected of them. Their life has order and purpose. Having experienced nothing else, they don't realize how fortunate they are.

Then they graduate college, and suddenly the train tracks they hadn't even realized they were riding on fall away. Where once they had milestones and goals set out for them, now there is nothing. A big question mark seems to float over life. It is as though we are all Wiley Coyotes, charging up a cliff. Suddenly, the cliff is gone and for one terrifying second of uncertainty, we hang there in midair, a look of "what now?" plastered on our faces.

This is a time more liberating than any you have ever known before, and it is both exciting and terrifying in its freedom. Suddenly, life is undefined, and everything seems open to you. No one is handing you assignments anymore; the only assignments now are the ones you choose to undertake. It is a realization more intense than any stimulant. I remember the first time this realization hit me.

It had been a week since I graduated. The preceding days had been filled with non-stop celebration and partying with my friends. My family even got into the action, taking me out to dinner. Accolades and praise rained down on me from every corner, from everyone, even distant relatives I never knew I had and friends I'd long ago forgotten. My bank account did quite nicely over this interval as the checks stapled to congratulatory cards piled in.

Things started to calm down after about a week, and I found myself lounging about my room one lazy afternoon. I don't know what sparked it, but suddenly the question popped into my head: What now?

I paused. "What now?" I repeated to myself. Suddenly, I sat up, shivers running down my spine, as the realization hit: I had no idea. All the order and structure I had known was suddenly gone, and I had no idea what to replace it with. I had been so focused on getting through college that I had given almost no thought to what I would do afterwards. I panicked a little as the uncertainty of my situation dawned on me.

I sat down with my parents that night and talked it over. With a wisdom born out of experience, they managed to calm me down. We would begin looking for jobs the next day.

I wasn't entirely sure what I wanted to do, but making money seemed like a pretty important criterion to a guy in his early twenties. My degree, a Bachelor's in General Studies, left a lot of options open for me to potentially pursue, and I explored a number of positions in different fields.

After several weeks of searching, something finally caught my interest. It was an entry-level position at a financial services firm. If you were accepted into the program, you worked for them for a year or two, gathering on-the-job experience and training as you went along. At the end of that time, the firm tested you, and if you did well, you were sent out on your own to open and run a branch in another part of the city.

The very fact that this job would involve a lot of math should have set off warning bells for me. Unfortunately, the prospect of a lucrative career and being my own boss in only a few short years proved too tempting for me to pass up. I applied and was accepted into the program.

The work proved repetitive and dull, and I was never able to grasp the complexities of the financial business practice. I got by mainly by the strength of my personality and a not insignificant amount of bluffing. Then exam time rolled around, and the corporate world proved far less accommodating than my later schooling had been. The test mercilessly probed my deficiencies; it was in written format and required odious amounts of math. I couldn't bluff my way out of this one.

When my manager received my results, his first incredulous comment to me was, "Marcus," (he seemed to like calling me that), "what were you smoking all through college?" I had failed the test and failed it badly. I tried to explain to him the nature of my learning disability but found a very unsympathetic audience. Red flags immediately went up on my account; the firm had recognized me as a bad investment and immediately sought to cut its losses. In a matter of days, I was "asked" to look elsewhere for employment.

This experience, though ultimately a futile one that wasted a year of my life, taught me an important lesson. I had been under no delusions that math was anything other than my Achilles heel. Basic college algebra had stumped me on numerous occasions and almost prevented me from graduating college. As you recall, I ended up graduating not because I finally mastered the material, but because I found a non-math equivalent to take instead. To think that I could have a successful career in a field that would require extensive calculating and numerical manipulation seems positively foolish now. Back then, it didn't.

Flush from the success of graduating college, I had an unreasonable notion of my own talents. There was nothing I couldn't do, I figured, so long as I worked hard enough at it. So when I found this tantalizing job prospect, I told myself I would do it. It would be tough, but I was driven to succeed and had a good work ethic; how could I not succeed?

There is a famous saying, "Know thyself." I may have known myself at this time, but I chose to ignore it. As a result, rather than looking for a career more suited to my strengths, I looked for careers that would maximize my earning potential, regardless of how suited I was to them. It would take me many years and several false starts before I would finally take this lesson to heart.

The fallout from the financial services firm found me unemployed and once again directionless. This is not the way any man wants to spend his mid-twenties—the prime of his life spent in the unemployment line. I wouldn't say I fell into depression at this point, but the lack of direction in my life proved very destructive. I put on weight during this time, not really caring about my appearance or health. I also began drinking fairly heavily at this juncture, partying regularly with my friends. That alcohol served as an escape for me, I have no doubt, but primarily, I drank because I had nothing better to do.

I was a man in need of direction, and I turned to a center that provided occupational counseling. I would meet with a counselor there every week, and the advice he offered me forever altered my life for the better.

The first thing he emphasized was that a successful life on the job required a successful life off it. He told me straight out that my constant partying was going to have negative consequences, and that if I did not curtail it soon, I was going to be condemning myself to alcoholism down the road. Of course I scoffed that off; there was no way I would ever become dependent on alcohol. I did it recreationally, I told him. I wasn't dependent on drinking and would have no problem stopping if needed. Reading this, you are probably laughing at how cliché I sounded; haven't these denials be trotted out by substance abusers the world over? The truth is that no matter how clichéd, I genuinely believed it.

My counselor did something brilliant to wake me up to the fact that I was developing a problem. He had me start keeping a journal of my activities, recording when I drank and how much I consumed. We'll explore in depth why this was so effective later on, but looking over that journal, with the irrefutable evidence of how pervasive alcohol had become in my life staring back at me, I realized he was right, and I immediately began cutting back.

For my career, the counselor told me that at this stage I had to establish myself as a reputable and desirable candidate to perspective employers, and to do so, I needed to earn certifications. To this end, I enrolled in an occupational vocation rehabilitation program and studied for a real estate certification. The material was fairly straightforward, but unsurprisingly, the certification test proved too taxing for me the first time around. After some cajoling, I convinced them to administer it to me orally a second time, and in this format, where someone read the questions to me and I dictated the answers, I easily passed.

Armed with my newfound credentials, I soon found work at a local real estate agency, managing properties and brokering deals. It wasn't the most exciting of work, but it gave my life the purpose it had recently lacked. My life was starting to turn around. I was earning a steady living now in a respectable field. Physically, things were also improving. I was working out again and losing weight. It wasn't a thrilling time, but at least my life was on track.

Welcome to the Corporate World—Lessons

Should you take nothing else from this book, should my advice in every other section be ignored entirely, take away this, arguably the single most important thing I have to offer: in life, the key to finding true happiness and success is to **know thyself**.

What this advice calls on you to do is simply to endeavor to truly understand who are. Understand what motivates you and what inspires you to greatness. Learn where your strengths and weakness lie. Figure out where your strengths and, more important, your deficiencies exist. In short, **be completely honest to yourself about who you are.**

As I stated in the story, at this stage in my life, I did not know myself, and many of the mistakes I made during this time were the result of it. I had many delusions about myself, and these delusions clouded my judgment, not allowing me to correctly analyze situations.

The first of these delusions was an **unfounded sense of ability,** stated otherwise as **not knowing one's own limits**. We had talked last chapter about being your own best advocate and the troubles that can result from not believing in yourself. Here we are focusing on the other extreme, of believing in yourself too much. A healthy ego is both important and necessary for success, but an ego can become too bloated, and delusion can result.

Should an ego become this bloated, one begins to believe himself capable of practically anything. The world is this person's oyster; there is nothing he can't do. This is an extreme, but on more realistic levels, with individual talents or situations, this sort of delusion occurs constantly.

If you have ever seen auditions for shows like *American Idol* you will immediately see how destructive yet prevalent this delusion is. People completely devoid of even the semblance of talent go before the judges, absolutely convinced they are this country's next great as yet undiscovered talent. To their complete surprise, the judges flatly reject them. Their subsequent outbursts of grief and anger feed a guilty pleasure of watching these types of shows, enjoying a laugh at those deluded people's expense.

But while monotonic, off-key singers thinking themselves the next great singing divas might be extreme examples, we are all guilty of similar delusions from time to time. In fact, these sorts of delusions occur almost daily and are a constant part of our lives. The man who thinks he can tee off from the professional distance and hit the fairway; the woman who thinks she can finish the presentation and balance her department's expense sheets in time to pick up her kids from school; the man who, looking to impress a date, tries to cook her a Cajun dish he has never even heard of before, are all examples of times when we foster delusions about our own abilities. Every day, on numerous undertakings, we overestimate our abilities.

Almost always, the consequences of these miscalculations are miniscule. A lost ball; having to call the husband to pick the kids up instead; ordering in Chinese food, all the while fumigating the apartment in a desperate attempt to get rid of the smoky stench, are hardly worth devoting a self-help section to. Occasionally though, these delusions are bigger, and the consequences of following them are much more severe.

An example of this sort of delusion was clearly on display when I took the financial services job. I simply am not cut out to work in finance, yet

I deluded myself into thinking I could. This delusion ended up wasting much of my early twenties, costing me precious years of development.

It is important to have ambitions in life and to keep working toward bettering yourself. Equally important though is to be realistic in those ambitions. Recklessly setting goals you are simply incapable of accomplishing only sets you up for failure in the future. Therefore, prior to undertaking any task of significance, try being as honest with yourself as you can about your ability to accomplish it. If you are genuinely incapable of succeeding, don't let yourself become deluded into thinking otherwise. You will only end up hurting yourself for it.

It is a level of maturity in outlook that does not easily develop, but the sooner you do develop it, the better off you'll be. Many of the mistakes I made early in adulthood resulted from the delusions of myself I held. It took me many years—and even till this day I struggle to be completely realistic and honest with myself. The ability to be more self-critical will be crucial to success.

There is a second form of delusion that we are all guilty of from time to time, one that is arguably even more harmful to our well-being. This form of delusion is opposite from the first in its effect, in that it does not encourage undertaking destructive behavior; rather, it prevents us from stopping destructive behavior once it's begun. It is so potent that at times, even when the negative effects of an action become obvious to everyone else around us, we ignore them entirely. This form of delusion is known as **denial.**

Note that denial is not what causes the problem, at least not at first. Denial's function is to worsen existing problems we might have by preventing us from realizing just how damaging they are. Denial fogs our perception of reality, deluding us into believing that everything is all right. In extremes of denial, our perception can become so distorted that it no longer even resembles reality.

Denial almost ruined my life. I was headed down a dangerous path to alcoholism and I refused to acknowledge it. Though I didn't see it at the time, drinking was becoming a refuge from reality for me. It wasn't that I had anything to run away from; I just had nothing else to run to. Drinking slowly began to define my life; I lived for the parties, the bar outings, the clubbing. Nothing else seemed to matter.

In hindsight, it is readily apparent why this was so dangerous. Alcohol can be a fun and even healthy diversion when consumed in moderation; millions of Americans consume it regularly with no adverse consequences. The trick is that alcohol should only be a diversion; it should never be the primary goal. For instance, when you go out, if you go out to be with friends and drinking is simply what your group decides to do, that is a healthy outlook. Alcohol becomes dangerous, though, when it becomes the central motivation. When you start drinking to drink, and you start defining your fun as getting drunk, this sets up a mental attitude that can become so dangerous later on.

So how does denial arise? How was I so blind to what was happening to me? The field of psychology has a theory called **cognitive dissonance theory** that I think goes a long way toward explaining how denial arises. Cognitive dissonance discusses what happens to a person when he regularly engages in activities he is uncomfortable with. The classic example of this might be a torturer, someone who, for whatever reason, must torture people, but is very uncomfortable with the idea of torture. This condition is termed cognitive dissonance, where a person's actions and ideals are out of alignment, and resultantly, the person is very uncomfortable with his status.

The theory states that a person will naturally seek to bring his actions out of conflict with his ideals. There are two ways this happens: either the action changes to match the ideal, or the outlook changes to match the action. New Year's resolutions are an easy example of how we alter our actions to match our ideals. Smoking is often an example of the opposite.

Smokers are people who often face cognitive dissonance. They must reconcile how they justify constantly using a product that will cause adverse health effects down the road and not infrequently might kill them. To bring an ideal into alignment with action, a smoker will often come to redefine acceptable health. Who hasn't had conversations with smokers where they tell you, "So what if I get cancer when I'm seventy? Seventy is a long life, and smoking calms me down now."

This process occurs constantly, from the person who stops attending church regularly to the child who no longer calls her parents daily. We will constantly shift our priorities and standards in order for them to better reflect our actions. The consequence of this is that even standards we would have once thought deplorable become acceptable to us over time, and actions we might at one time have never considered doing become standard, daily routines.

Applying this to my story, the more I began to drink, the more my perceptions of alcohol abuse shifted, till I no longer found my actions in any way inappropriate or harmful. As a result, denial set in, and I saw no problem with what I was doing.

So how does one extricate him or herself from this hole? After all, if one doesn't even believe he has a problem (as I didn't), what is to motivate the person to even look to change? There is a reason why substance abuse programs always say admitting the problem is the first step.

Often that is the biggest hurdle—recognizing that your perceptions have become flawed.

What I recommend for you is what worked for me: a process I call **third-person introspection**. Essentially, what you need to do in order to escape denial is to examine yourself the way a stranger would, critically and without any internal bias. Judge yourself as you would a stranger, and not surprisingly, you will find yourself far more honest in your assessment.

This is easily said, but how is it carried out? The trick that worked for me was to **separate the observation from the judgment**. Observe and record your actions first, and then later examine and critique your actions. This took the form of a journal of my daily activities my counselor suggested I start keeping. I observed and recorded all my actions as I went along, and only later did I look over it and analyze my life. But though I had written and experienced everything in that journal, somehow reading it distanced me from the actual events, and I found I was able to examine it objectively, as though I was exploring someone else's life. When placed in this mindset, the fog of denial lifted, and I began to see irrefutably how destructive my actions were becoming. It might seem contradictory, but sometimes in order to **know thyself** best, you have to step out of yourself and become a stranger.

It may be ancient advice that has been handed down for generations, but it is no less relevant today. Know thyself, honestly and completely. Hold no delusions about your abilities and deficits, and honestly asses your status in life. It is the hardest thing in the world to be truly honest with yourself, for we lie so often and easily to ourselves. But if you can fight the temptation to delude yourself and can face life clearly, you will end up for better for it.

To summarize this section:

- **Know thyself**. Strive to be as honest and complete as possible in your understanding of who you are and what you need.

- **Avoid delusion.** Don't fall for the easy temptation to distort your situation both by avoiding **denial** and **an underserved sense of ability.**

- **Apply third-person introspection** on yourself should you suspect that your ideals might be distorted. Do this by separating observation from judgment, allowing you to critically examine your actions.

Chapter 5:
A Life Redefined

In this chapter:

Story-The Accident and Its Aftermath
Lessons-Hillel's Three Challenges

A Life Redefined

In a moment, everything can change. One minute we're plodding along in our lives, wistfully oblivious to the tenuous state of life, when suddenly everything that had till now defined us can abruptly and jarringly be shattered. It is the sad irony of life, that intricate planning and elaborate execution are required to construct order and purpose, whereas destruction and chaos are so easily obtained. There can be no reckoning of if or when or how events like these will happen. You could be crossing a street on the way to work, your toaster's wiring could spark, a large morsel of food could get lodged in your throat, or, in my case, you could be driving to a real estate auction.

It was the sort of August day that deludes one into thinking Pittsburgh weather is actually tolerable. It was a clear and beautiful day—warm enough, without being oppressively so. The drive was uneventful, with just enough traffic to make it a hassle. The radio was playing the sort of songs that were tolerable enough to not justify changing the channel, but hardly the kind that beg to be sung aloud with the windows rolled down. It was completely bland, beautiful, and normal in every possible respect, the kind of day that lulls a person into complacency—exactly the kind of day when something life-altering would occur.

Although it was the weekend, I was still working. Sundays were when many auctions were held, and that day I was slated to attend a real estate auction in Pittsburgh's South Side and bid on a couple of commercial properties my firm had been eyeing. Others in the office tended to hate field trips, but I loved being away from my desk and always volunteered when possible. Eventually, my managers wised up and started handing me the brunt of the fieldwork, so eventually, working weekends had become typical.

I merged onto the parkway that whipped by downtown, a commute that affords one exquisite views of both the downtown and the Monongahela riverfront. When my exit came, I turned onto the Liberty Bridge, which crossed the river and fed into the Liberty Tunnel, one of Pittsburgh's numerous tunnels carved into the foothills of the Allegheny Mountains.

In the years following the accident, I have tried to blame the driver numerous times but have never been able to. How can one fault a man for trying to push himself a little longer, a little later, desperate to get home and spend some time with his family? That probably wasn't the first time he had pulled an all-night shift, and for all I know, he had never messed up before, but on that day, at that time, on that road, he fell asleep at the wheel of a pickup truck.

I first noticed the truck in my rearview mirror as it began to barrel down on me. Beginning to get uncomfortable with the closing gap between him and myself, I applied the gas, but soon found myself up against the car in front of me. I looked back, and the truck kept coming. I was in a tunnel, and had no readily available means of getting out of the way. I probably should have honked, but in the heat of the moment, the only thing I could do was brace myself for what I still couldn't quite believe was about to happen.

Accelerating the car was probably the only reason I survived and was not flattened by the runaway pickup; that was perhaps the best thing I can say about the accident. The truck plowed into me full speed, crushing the rear of my car and carrying me into the rear bumper of the car in front of me. The full force of a speeding truck was transferred into my car, crushing it in a destructive sandwich of metal, fuel, and leather. My head was thrown backward, and I suffered rather severe whiplash.

The adrenaline from the crash kept me conscious and aware in the aftermath of the crash. A passer by phoned 911 and a stood around in a daze until the ambulance arrived to transport me to the hospital. Miraculously, it seemed I had gone largely uninjured in the accident. I had a couple minor cuts and bruises as well as the whiplash, but that was the extent of my injuries. They kept me in observation for a couple of hours, but after no new problems emerged, they released me.

Unfortunately, my troubles hadn't yet been realized. Kind of like the aftermath of an intense workout, I didn't really feel the pain until the next morning. When I woke up the following morning, my neck was incredibly sore, and I could barely move it. I went back to the hospital, where a neurologist confirmed that I had suffered severe neck trauma and would have to be put on immediate, intense rehabilitation.

I requested a couple days off from work, and they were quickly granted. Those next few days would prove transformative. By all accounts I was lucky to be alive, and as everyone who has gone through a near-death experience knows, you never feel as alive as you do in the days that follow. Every breath you take is a gift of unimaginable proportion; every step you make is endowed with unparalleled meaning; life is more beautiful than you have ever realized.

These days would also be very contemplative ones for me. Up till this point, death had just been an abstract idea. I knew I was going to die someday; I had just never really internalized my own mortality. Some people implicitly do; they just get how fragile life is. For me, it took a near-death experience for my very mortality to become apparent. For the first time, I realized that life was a short and precious commodity, and I had till this point wasted it on foolish and unsatisfying endeavors.

In chapter three, we spoke about the need to focus on ends. Well, for the first time, I focused on mine. I realized then that real estate was not my calling; I was not going to be happy spending my life in that field, and I began to look around for an alternative.

At the time, I was in intensive physical therapy for my neck. It was the first time I had really been a patient, and it gave me a new perspective on the health services field. I had always loved the outdoors and athletics, and I began to wonder if I could turn my passion into a career. During my physical therapy sessions, I grilled my poor therapist ceaselessly about the field, wanting to know exactly what sort of options there were for me. He suggested that I look into personal training, and after exploring the requirements for certification, I decided to pursue it.

There is the unfortunate perception of personal training as the simple memorization and regurgitation of a few workout routines. To believe this though would be akin to believing that all a doctor does is memorize a few tests to perform on patients. Personal training, when done correctly, requires that the trainer possess an intimate knowledge of the human anatomy and a detailed understanding of its physiology. The ability to correctly prescribe proper workouts depends on having the proper level of understanding of the human body; otherwise, the workout suggested might end up doing more harm than good.

Furthermore, before the trainer even begins working out clients, he must first evaluate his client physically, determining areas that need improvement, be it aerobic conditioning, strength training, toning, etc. Often, especially after injury, there are specific muscles or joints that must be targeted. Once problem areas are identified, the personal trainer then has to discuss goals with the client. The ironman competitor will have a very different set of goals than a busy professional looking to shed some weight and tone up. Once those are determined, the personal trainer then has to assess the logistics of implementing a workout regimen. Variables, like the time that can be devoted to it and the equipment available, must all be factored in.

Only then can a personal trainer begin to custom fit a program to maximize an individual client's needs. The better the trainer, the better the program he designs. A personal trainer must also act as a constant motivator, pushing the client to new physical limits to which he wouldn't dream to take himself. A personal trainer may also occasionally be called upon to be a mentor, a therapist, a marriage counselor, a coach, and most important, a friend.

It is a challenging field to be sure, but in personal training, I had discovered my passion. I went on to take the course and received certification.

By now though I had learned an important lesson when it came to earning a living: never put all your eggs in one basket. I realized that if I were to be successful, I would need to be as diverse in my offerings as possible. Therefore, I got in touch with a local tennis pro. He taught me the game and how to instruct it. I studied with him and, within a year, was able to get certified as a tennis instructor.

I also returned to hockey at this time, the passion of my youth. I had already been licensed to referee hockey for several years, but now I wanted to get into the coaching side of it as well. At this time, I received an in-line skating instructional certificate.

By the time I was done with slew of "certififying," as my family called it, I had also received certification as a therapeutic masseuse practitioner. If these couple years ever made it into a Chinese calendar, I have no doubt they would be the Year of the Certification.

Having now amassed a respectable portfolio, I began to market myself. At this time, my day job, as it were, was selling eyeglasses. Working around this nine-to-five, slowly I began to amass a clientele and started working for local fitness centers and even the city of Pittsburgh. Referrals began to trickle in and opened up new venues for me, and I began to work in afterschool programs and senior centers.

As my business is the sort that relies almost exclusively on referrals, it took a couple of years for it to start gaining enough momentum that I could do it full time. Eventually, though, I was able to make the jump, switching first to part-time at the eyeglass center; and then, finally, one wonderful morning, I tended my resignation to the store. My years in corporate America were finally over.

I now do this full-time. It is a true joy to combine my passion for sports and my outgoing nature with a successful career. The nineties hit movie *Office Space* posed the now-famous question, "If you had a million dollars, what would you do?" If I had one million dollars, I would do exactly what I am doing right now. (Though thanks to inflation, one million probably isn't enough nowadays, but the point is still relevant.) It is such a satisfying feeling to wake up every morning, excited for the day ahead. There are challenging days to be certain, but here, now, I feel as though I am genuinely making a difference in the lives of others.

But I have always been one to look forward, and looking forward I realized that my personal training has given me numerous opportunities to mentor children and adults, and that, coupled with my life experiences, has afforded me the unique ability to help guide people through obstacles in their lives. Therefore, I went back to school yet again, and immediately prior to sitting down to work on this book, I became certified as a life coach.

Enough about my life though; let's talk some more about yours.

A Life Redefined-Lessons

The accident served as a wakeup call to me, a not so subtle cue to focus my life on my passions. I may have needed something as drastic as an accident to wake me up, but hopefully it won't take anything nearly so dire for you.

We have talked in preceding sections on how and when to change life directions to fit priorities, but what we never focused on is what those priorities should actually be. This is perhaps the most critical element for a successful life transformation, for if you shift for the wrong reasons, you will often find yourself no better than you were before. The question therefore then becomes, what should your priorities be?

There is much advice written about this, with each so called expert telling you exactly what your priorities ought to be. Some will tell you to focus on what you enjoy doing, others to not prioritize the earning of money, and virtually all will tell you to put family first. I however will endeavor to not do this. It is not that I do not find their advice or suggestions wrong, but merely that it would be wrong for me to subjectively tell you what your priorities should be.

The simple fact is that there is no correct answer to where your priorities should lie. Everyone's will naturally fall out differently. For some, family and children will always come first, while for others, settling down and raising a family isn't even something they want. Some will find fulfillment in work, others in enjoying life. We can make subjective judgment on the merits of certain priorities, but I will leave that to others. Let us instead focus on how to achieve yours, whatever they happen to be.

The ancient Jewish philosopher Hillel once famously asked three questions that I think accurately summarize this section. He asked, "**If you are not for yourself, who will be? But if you are only for yourself, what are you? And if not now, when?**" These three questions, posed as a challenge to my ancestors, I now turn around and pose to you.

If you are not for yourself, who will be? As you will recall, this question parallels advice I gave a couple of chapters ago, when I asked you to be your own best advocate. Building on that, as well as on the need to focus on ends that we have also discussed, the question we must now ask is what your priorities should be; what are the ends which you should strive to see accomplished?

The simple and rather obvious answer is that your priorities should be your own. If you wish to be truly happy it is crucial that you discover what is important to you and live your life it its pursuit. **Live your life according to your priorities; life is far too short to waste it on anything else.**

Introspection is required here. We had talked before about meditating to focus on attaining ends; now I'm asking you more fundamentally to meditate on what your ends should be. Take the time to critically ask yourself what excites you, what gives you fulfillment, what do you look forward to doing. In short, identify your passions.

Sports would prove to be mine, and I have found my life enriched by their pursuit. For others, passion can take numerous forms. Helping people, earning money, children, medicine, politics, animals—what is your passion? The answer to that question is what you should devote your life to.

This is easier said than done. There are surprisingly many ways in which our priorities get skewed. The most common is that **we allow others to define them for us.** This happens so often in life; most times, we probably do not even realize it. Essentially, this occurs every time we do something we otherwise wouldn't in order to satisfy the wishes of someone else. Everything from getting a haircut to please the wife, to applying to college because of your parent's wishes, is an example of your priorities being set by others.

Of course, as with most things, this isn't all bad. To the contrary, part of living with others and getting along with them is making sacrifices for them. Compromise is critical to friendships and relationships, and the ability to be flexible to the needs of others is a very laudable trait. We will discuss this in greater detail when we explore Hillel's second question. For the present though, I will clarify an important distinction between laudable compromise and inadvisable compromise when it comes to prioritization. Prioritizing the needs of others is laudable; prioritizing other's priorities for you, over your own, is not.

This second scenario is what I wish to focus on. It can happen that your entire life comes to be defined by others. For whatever reason, your desires are ignored entirely in your decision making process. You have become completely beholden to the wishes and demands of others.

It is obvious how unsatisfying a life like this is. Your entire life is lived essentially as a servant, in the service of other's desires. None of your goals will be attained, none of your passions pursued. This clearly is not a life that will leave you feeling happy and fulfilled.

The critical distinction of why this compromise is bad is that your priorities are not defined by anyone else's needs (for instance taking the highest paying job in order to best provide for your family), but rather simply done to satisfy someone else's vision of who you should be (for instance, cleaning up your look because your girlfriend would want you to look more respectable). Although they might be happier to see you morph to fit their image of you, ultimately, the only person this change will affect will be you.

Understanding this, the question is then where does a proper balance lay, a balance between being receptive to the needs of others all the while being able to pursue your own goals. When does simply being agreeable interfere with your ability to enjoy life?

To answer this, I would once again call on the **test of permanence**, only this time, I would ask that you apply it to yourself.

The test of permanence, again, is where you ask yourself what the consequences of a course of action will be. If the consequences are ultimately trivial, it is wise to be flexible to others; on the other hand, should the consequences be life-defining, you must be able to put your priorities first or risk living a life not your own.

Examples of trivial things might include what you eat for dinner or what you wear on a night out on the town. You are not likely to remember them even a week later, and certainly they will hardly alter the course of your life. Therefore, if there is someone who feels passionately about this, someone you care for as either a friend, lover, family member, or business colleague, it would behoove you to be flexible in these areas. Ultimately, it will make you a more pleasant companion.

On the other hand if the consequences are life-altering, selfishness needs to be displayed. A clear example of this might be where (or even if) you go to college. Often, you will receive pressure from parents and family as to which school to go to or what field to major in. If you allow them to chose your fate, you resign your life to living as they would want you to. Your life is no longer yours and is now your parents' desires played out by you.

In life, the opinions of others are important, but none are more important than your own. If you are not happy with what others are forcing you to do, why would you do it? Don't let yourself become a slave to the whims of others; your life is too valuable to spend in the pursuit of any goals other than your own. When it comes to yourself, be selfish.

Sometimes though, we are our worst enemy in this regard. We have passions, yes, but we convince ourselves that, for whatever reason, they are impractical. When we are children, our world is filled with our dreams. We will be astronauts, police officers, scientists, and doctors. Life is our canvass; it merely waits for us to apply the paint. Then we leave Never-Never Land, and we grow older. Suddenly, our dreams are pushed aside by what we view as practicalities. Dreams have no place for an adult, we tell ourselves, and we ignore them.

I was like this once. Working real estate was a sensible and practical decision on my part. My life was orderly and secure; I was no longer the mess I had been earlier. There was nothing that forced me to change. Had I continued, I would have gone on to live a pleasant life. But is pleasant really good enough when all we get is one chance, one life? If your answer is no, why do you accept mediocrity for yourself? **If you are not for yourself, who will be?**

Hillel's second challenge to us was: **If you are only for yourself, what are you?** What he was telling us was to remember that no one in this world is an island; we are all connected and are all dependent on one another. Every one of us needs other people and have other people who need us.

This need can take material form, the way your children require you to provide for them as an example. It can also take psychological form. A friend will need you to comfort him in a time of tragedy; a family member will need you to spend time with her and show her the nurturing love she will need in order to get by.

The reality of life is that you will always have others who will depend on you. If you ignore them, Hillel asks, what sort of person does that make you?

To be selfish here, at the expense of those who need you most, is an act so deplorable I cannot begin to criticize it harshly enough. To neglect those dependent on you is to abandon the very things that make you human. If you do not wish to bear the needs of others, do not forge any bonds that would cause dependence. Do not make friends; do not have a family. If, for instance, you are unwilling to take the time to be there for your children, do not have them. Once you have them, though, you simply cannot neglect them. **Their needs must become your own, and their well-being must become your priority.** If it does not, then what are you?

Hillel's final challenge to us, **if not now, when?**, is a call to action. There is truth to the adage that tells us that **there is no time like the present**. If you have a dream or passion that is till now unrealized, or if you have till now been negligent in your care for others, he is telling you that it is never too early or too late to change. There will never be an ideal time to change; there will always be holdups and challenges, always reasons to delay. Hillel is telling us to move in spite of the challenges.

If you have a dream, a passion, **find a way to make it a reality.** You might not earn as much, and you might have to work longer hours in the process, but if you work hard and intelligently enough, I can almost guarantee you this: you will succeed. Consider this thought, whatever your passion is: I can almost guarantee you others share it, others who can go from fellow enthusiasts to customers, so long as you're willing to put yourself out there. Remember, **if not now, when?**

If you have neglected your family or friends, it is never too late to change. Do not let complacency and fear prevent you from reaching out to those who need you the most. It is never too late, and no wound is ever too deep to be mended. Remember Hillel's advice: **if not now, when?**

To summarize this chapter:

- **If you are not for yourself, who will be?**

- **Live your life according to your priorities and passions;** the happiest people are the ones who pursue their dreams.

- **Take the time to define what your passions are and figure out a practical way to make them a reality.**

- **Don't let others define your priorities for you.**

- **Don't fall victim to the idea that you are too old or mature to pursue dreams.**

- **If you are only for yourself, what are you?**

- **Make the needs of those who depend on you your priority.** Others need you and depend on you for love, guidance, and support. Do not neglect those who you have allowed to become dependent on you.

- **If not now, when?** There will never be a time like the present. **Realize that there will always be hardships in undertaking a change.** There will never be a perfect time.

- **It is never too late, and no wound is irreparable.** Reach out to those who need you, even if till now you have not.

Chapter 6:
The Power of Sports

In this chapter:

-The Power and Promise of Sports

The Power of Sports

There is something magical about walking onto a basketball court. Crossing that foul line transports you into another universe. The rules that have governed you till now no longer apply. Here, you are no longer a mid-level manager of an industrial supply company, a parent, a brother, a little league coach; here, all you are now is a point guard. Here you cannot fall back on your previous successes, and none of your real world failures will dog you. Your concerns vanish; the mortgage, the kid's schooling, the politics at the office no longer matter. For the next hour, your only passion, your entire life's purpose, is getting an inflated rubber-and-paint ball through an elevated ring as often as possible, all the while preventing your opponents from doing the same. In this parallel universe, friends can become adversaries and strangers can become instant allies. For one joyous hour, you are living a different existence; it is vacation more intense than you could ever hope to buy.

Then the hour ends, and like a fairytale princess at midnight, we revert back to our normal lives, with only the memories of past glories and the vague promise of future visits to this universe to sustain us. We walk slowly to the locker room, shower, and change costumes to better fit the universe of life. Walking out the door of the gym, we become seemingly indistinguishable from the people scurrying around us.

That sports is an entertaining and often necessary diversion is unquestionable, but is that all this parallel universe we call sports is, a simple outlet from the stresses of the real world? Are sports only a simple game, fundamentally unimportant to life? Having devoted my life to fitness and sports, I can resoundingly assure you they are anything but.

Sports and life are not nearly as separate as I may have first implied. The two universes feed off one another, and a lesson learned in one can be powerfully applied to the other. As a result, it would be a grave error to ignore the positive roll sports can play in your life. It is this idea that I wish to explore in this chapter.

First let us examine the most apparent and readily understandable benefit of sports: **the physical benefits of exercise**. The health benefits of regularly engaging in physical activity have been so long established that we would be hard pressed to find a child in this country who did not know that working out is healthy for him or her. Nevertheless, given how few Americans get enough exercise, it is worth repeating.

Regular exercise has been shown to reduce the incidence and severity of chronic diseases. Exercise has been proven to promote healthy blood sugar levels that can help **prevent or control diabetes.**[1] It has also been shown to promote bone density to help protect against **osteoporosis.**[2] People who exercise regularly have a lower overall risk of developing **cancer.**[3] Exercise has proven the ideal way to increase levels of HDL (High Density Lipoprotein) or "good" cholesterol, all while reducing blood pressure, lowering the risk of developing **heart disease.**[4]

Exercise has also been shown to improve mental health. A study conducted at Duke University studied people suffering from **depression** and found that 60 percent of participants who exercised regularly overcame their depression without using antidepressant medication.[5]

---

[1] BUPA Insurance Online, "Health Benefits of Exercise," http://www.nutristrategy.com/health.htm.

[2] Ibid.

[3] Ibid.

[4] Mayo Clinic Online, "Exercise: 7 benefits of regular physical activity," http://www.mayoclinic.com/health/exercise/HQ01676.

[5] Find Counseling, "Mental Health Benefits of Exercise," http://www.findcounseling.com/journal/health-fitness/.

To give you an idea of how effective that is, that was about the same successful percentage rate as those who only used medication in their treatment for depression. Even those who do not suffer from depression have been shown to benefit mentally from exercise. The release of endorphins during and immediately after a workout has been shown to reduce **stress and anxiety.**[6]

On top of all that, exercise has been proven to increase immune response, keeping you from getting sick as often. It improves sleep, and has even been shown to boast one's sex life[7]. Yet in spite of all these apparent benefits, millions of Americans do not get the exercise they need.

So how do I know if I'm getting enough exercise? The World Health Organization estimates that the minimum level of physical activity required to maintain health, for someone eighteen years old and above, is **thirty minutes of moderate activity five times per week,** or, **twenty minutes of intensive activity three times a week.**[8]

---

[6] Mayo.
[7] Ibid.
[8] World Health Organization, "Recommended Amount of Physical Activity," http://www. who.int/dietphysicalactivity/factsheet_recommendations/en/index.html.

The following table, from the WHO site, details what activities constitute moderate and intense activity:

Moderate-intensity Physical Activity (Approximately 3-6 METs) Requires a moderate amount of effort and noticeably accelerates the heart rate.	Vigorous-intensity Physical Activity (Approximately >6 METs) Requires a large amount of effort and causes rapid breathing and a substantial increase in heart rate.
Examples of moderate-intensity exercises include: -Brisk walking -Dancing -Gardening -Housework and domestic chores -Traditional hunting and gathering -Active involvement in games and sports with children/ walking domestic animals -General building tasks (e.g. roofing, thatching, painting) -Carrying/moving moderate loads (<20kg)	*Examples of vigorous-intensity exercise include:* -Running -Walking/Climbing briskly up a hill -Fast cycling -Competitive sports and games (e.g. Traditional games, Football, Volleyball, Hockey, Basketball) -Heavy shoveling or digging ditches -Carrying/moving heavy loads (>20kg)

If you are not getting at least this amount of exercise weekly, you are missing out on all the health benefits we mentioned above, and as a result are at a higher risk for the diseases and conditions we spoke of.

Improving your body by losing weight and toning up has benefits that go far beyond the physical. Feeling better about how you look will boost your self-confidence, reducing social anxiety and allowing you to become more assertive and outgoing. Studies have also shown that more attractive people tend to get listened to more often, and their opinions are held in higher regard. Furthermore, study after study has shown that attractive people earn significantly more than their less physically blessed peers. If these reasons aren't enough to convince you to get off the couch and go for a run, I'm not sure what will.

On top of all this though there is another benefit to sports that is easily overlooked, but I think is as, if not more, important. Sports, if properly utilized, can help foster proper personal development, and a proper sports program can actually cause success in life, improving on and building the skills necessary to succeed. Skeptical? Consider this following thought test.

Which of the following, sports or general living, require these for success:

- A focus on set goals

- Consistent determination and effort to see aims realized

- The ability to seize the initiative during times of adversity and not be afraid to take risks in order to see success realized

- Leadership to direct others to complete required objectives

- Dedication and commitment to seeing skills develop, laboring or practicing consistently on often laborious and repetitive tasks in order to gain proficiency

- The need to successfully interact with fellow humans, learning to work together to complete tasks, delegate responsibilities, and trust in colleagues to successfully complete their objectives

- The ability to handle success and, more important, to not allow defeat to get to you

- The talent to analyze situations properly and successfully implement strategies

- A little luck now and then

If you answered both, you would be correct. The unavoidable fact is that sports mirror life, and the skills one would need in order to become successful in sports can be applied to life. To get a better idea of how, let's examine each of the points in detail.

A focus on goals: In sports, goals are the only focus. All the dribbling skills in the world are useless if they don't translate into baskets. Likewise in football, a team can drive ninety yards, but if they turn over the ball at the one-yard line, all their effort was meaningless.

In life, goals are similarly the primary focus. This book focused heavily on identifying them and being able to carry those goals to realization. All the effort in this world, if not properly applied to the goals that one sets, will be ultimately futile and unfulfilling.

Consistent determination and effort to see aims realized: I have yet to encounter a sport where the first side to score wins. Most games are played over a set interval of time, with the winner being the one with the most at the end. Other games are played based on points, with the first to reach a certain amount of points winning. In both, consistent effort is required throughout. The baseball team that breaks out with a five-run lead in the first can easily lose it the very next inning if they do not consistently play hard. We read every day about fourth-quarter upsets or third-period comebacks. The team that does not consistently play well throughout a game will rarely be victorious.

Life will constantly be throwing challenges and obstacles at you, and if you only rise to meet them part of the time, the simple fact is you will not be successful. Life requires that you be on your A game 100 percent of the time. Life demands the discipline to continually and consistently fight through.

The ability to seize the initiative in times of adversity: In basketball, we refer to this as the clutch shot. Your team is down by two points with seven seconds left on the clock, yet in spite of the pressure, you call for the ball and take the shot for the win. This sort of behavior is the stuff of sports legend, the ability to rise to the pressure and overcome it.

How many corporate ventures have been saved by someone sticking his or her neck out, taking the risk and bringing the initiative to fruition? Life will constantly throw stressful obstacles at you. Someone might collapse in front of you, a professor might have just posed a question that no one wants to answer, a beautiful girl might be eyeing you at a bar—what do you do? Will you fold under the pressure and back down or will you rise to meet the occasion? Success comes to those who show up for it.

Leadership: Every team requires its leaders. They are the ones who can single-handedly spark a turnaround and lead the team to victory. They can be quarterbacks who execute a late fourth-quarter drive or they can be the guy who rallies the team from the bench. Leaders help a team through adversity and allow members to succeed by offering guidance and strength.

Effective leadership is held to the highest form of acclaim in life. Those who are capable of leading us through times of hardship, of guiding us and showing us how to reach success, are heralded as the heroes of our day. Let's not forget also that leaders tend to be well compensated for their services. Leadership is critical for success in life.

Dedication and commitment to seeing skills develop: Those who engage in sports competitively know that for every hour one actually spends in competition, that person will spend at least ten times as much time preparing for it. From weight training, to running, to the daily grind of practice, there is little excitement and thrill to the vast majority of sports. Virtually all the time given to athletics takes the form of daily monotonous routine.

The ones who succeed in this environment are the ones who develop the proper work ethic. They must be disciplined in their use of time and consistent in their habits. Contrary to the image of athletes as partying frat boys, the best athletes are often the hardest working and most disciplined of individuals.

This work ethic will be immensely useful in the real world. Most of life doesn't involve the intensity of the big moments but is comprised of the innumerable hours spent preparing for them. A properly developed work ethic will make one an effective professional or student. The discipline to plod through the grind of a daily routine is a skill of great value if properly developed.

People skills: Team sports can never be won by one individual. Eventually, one person will always be stopped; teams might need double or triple coverage to do it, but it will happen. Stars emerge only because they have a team to back them up. Learning to work with others, and relying on others to accomplish their end, is critical for success in sports.

In life, does the importance of people skills really require elaboration? From being able to network, to being able to effectively work with co-workers, people skills are critical to success. Individual stars might accomplish a lot in the real world, but eventually everyone will require the assistance of others.

The ability to handle both success and failure: Good sportsmanship is prized heavily in athletics. From the youngest T-ball leagues, we teach our athletes to always treat the other team with respect. We have the teams line up and shake hands following games, a reminder that ultimately it is only a game. We work to infuse this reality into our athletes, making them understand that a victory in a game is only that, but also that a defeat is simply a defeat in that game.

In life we tend to get carried away with the importance of certain things, getting an aggravated sense of their importance. It is important to be able to put everything into perspective, to not allow a single victory to let you become complacent and overly boastful and, more important, to not allow one setback to permanently cripple you.

Analyzing situations and implementing strategy: Although a lot of sports do revolve around physical action, there is an equally important mental side to competitive athletics as well. To ignore the role strategy plays in sports would be akin to looking at war as simple mindless combat. The best athletes aren't simply the most talented; they are the ones who are able to utilize their talent to achieve the maximum result, and this is done by strategically deploying the talent. Thus the best athletes must be able to correctly analyze the game situation, predicting outcomes and implementing strategies to best counter them.

Life similarly requires strategy. In order to be successful, one must be able to accurately analyze the situations one is immersed in and must be able to devise and implement strategies to best counter and overcome obstacles in life. All the talent in the world is useless if it is misapplied.

Examining these parallels, one can see why sports, if properly applied, can be a marvelous tool for molding success in life. The confidence gained on the court can translate into confidence in the real world. The dedication, focus, and meticulous attention to detail that training for sports requires will help develop a work ethic necessary for success. The courage to step up in times of adversity is what separates those who are remembered from those who simply were.

In my years of instructing sports, I have tried to instill these lessons in my clients, in the hopes that what they learn with me will be able to help them in all facets of life. People of every age can benefit from involvement in competitive athletics. For children, sports can help to develop their confidence and assertiveness. For students who struggle with their studies, sports can instill in them the focus and discipline necessary to excel at school. For adults, sports can engender the leadership and social skills necessary to get ahead.

So for my final piece of advice, I would tell you to **get involved.** Make the time for sports. Contrary to the idea that they are a diversion, sports could possibly be the most helpful extracurricular activity you undertake. In this hyper-competitive environment, parents looking to get their kids ahead should consider sports for them. The physical, mental, and educational benefits of athletics are virtually unparalleled. Few other activities can offer so much.

I say this not as someone who now sells sports, but as someone whose life has been forever improved by sports. Hockey was my sport, and it has given me more than I can ever hope to give it. Hockey imbued in me a confidence in my abilities, taught me leadership skills, helped me to face down adversity, and most important, showed me that I was capable of success at a time when I doubted myself. All I am today, I am on account of sports.

For those among us who are not athletically inclined, there is no reason for despair. The benefits of sports can be found in innumerable other activities. General fitness, running, swimming, and lifting regularly can also imbue many benefits. The physical benefits are chief among them, but discipline and work ethic can also successfully develop.

Other activities can also be equally instructive. The arts are a great parallel to sports. Performance art, for instance, requires dedication, discipline, stress management, and a certain amount of people skills. Although it might lack the strategic interplay sports incorporates, it is nonetheless a powerful tool for development as well.

This is true of most every hobby and interest. While some will be stronger at certain elements than others (chess, for instance, will have unparalleled strategic development, but lacks both physical and social skills benefits), almost every hobby can be helpful in fostering development. So again I urge you to **get involved** in whatever ultimately interests you and gather whatever skills from it you possibly can. **Diversion doesn't only have to be fun; it can also be crucial for development.**

To summarize this chapter:

- **Exercise is incredibly beneficial.** Both physically and mentally, athletics has been shown time and time again to be beneficial.

- **Sports can be an incredibly powerful tool for development.** Sports are an incredibly comprehensive and well-rounded activity, whose skills, if properly utilized, can be immeasurably helpful in the real world.

- **Get involved** Hobbies and extracurriculars of all sorts can be incredibly beneficial to development. They are not simply diversions.

Printed in the United States
204252BV00002B/418-444/P

9 781434 388254